MANDALA STONES

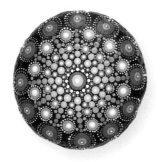

MANDALA STONES

Natasha Alexander

Search Press

A QUARTO BOOK

Published in 2017 by
Search Press Ltd
Wellwood
North Farm Road
Tunbridge Wells
Kent TN2 3DR

Reprinted 2018 (twice), 2019, 2020 (twice), 2021

ISBN: 978-1-78221-549-3

Conceived, designed and produced by
Quarto Publishing plc
The Old Brewery
6 Blundell Street
London N7 9BH
www.quartoknows.com

QUAR.MDSN

Editor: Victoria Lyle
Art editor and designer: Jackie Palmer
Photographer: Nicki Dowey
Editorial assistant: Danielle Watt
Art director: Caroline Guest
Creative director: Moira Clinch
Publisher: Samantha Warrington

Colour separation by Mission Repro
House, China
Printed in China by 1010 Printing International Limited.

CONTENTS

WELCOME TO MY WORLD

I first got into painting mandalas whilst on my healing journey from breast cancer, when I realised that I had ignored creativity as an important part of my life for too long and that it afforded me deep relaxation, which was needed for recovery. At first I thought I would be exploring creativity for a limited time. However, life had other ideas!

I was drawn back to mandalas time and again. There is something magical about them, aside from the endless glorious colour combinations and designs. In creating them, I find I'm in a state of deep, relaxing meditation and, because I'm loving what I'm doing, I'm also in a state of joy. It's a state where our ideas of limitations go quiet for an extended period of time and the organising principle of the Universe can start to bring us our desires. The consistent practice of making mandalas can literally turn our dreams into reality.

It's my experience that mandalas have the power to fascinate us; they contain a compelling, mysterious beauty, something that reaches deep into our being. This is a rarity in today's busy, information-driven world, which leaves a part of us yearning for something more. This 'something' is what the practice of creating mandalas has the power to nourish. It's an experience beyond the intellect and beyond words; it is something you will need to experience for yourself.

The mandala designs laid out for you to create in this book can be the beginning of a rewarding journey; mandalas may be based on the simple circle, but the designs you can create are infinite.

So my invitation, and my deepest desire for you, is that you will allow yourself some creative time and see what the practice of creating mandalas can yield. At the very least, you will be gifting yourself some meditative time for de-stressing, and at most, you might be transforming your world in ways that you cannot currently know, just like it did for me.

Happy mandala-ing!

Natasha

Moon Magic,
page 36

Winter Sunset,
page 38

Blossoms in the Wind,
page 40

MANDALA SELECTOR

This section shows all the mandalas in the book side by side so that you can quickly flick through, delight in all the different colours, patterns and designs, select the one you like best, then turn to the relevant page number for the instructions on how to create it.

Summer Meadow,
page 42

Fibonacci Glow,
page 44

Autumn's Gift, page 43

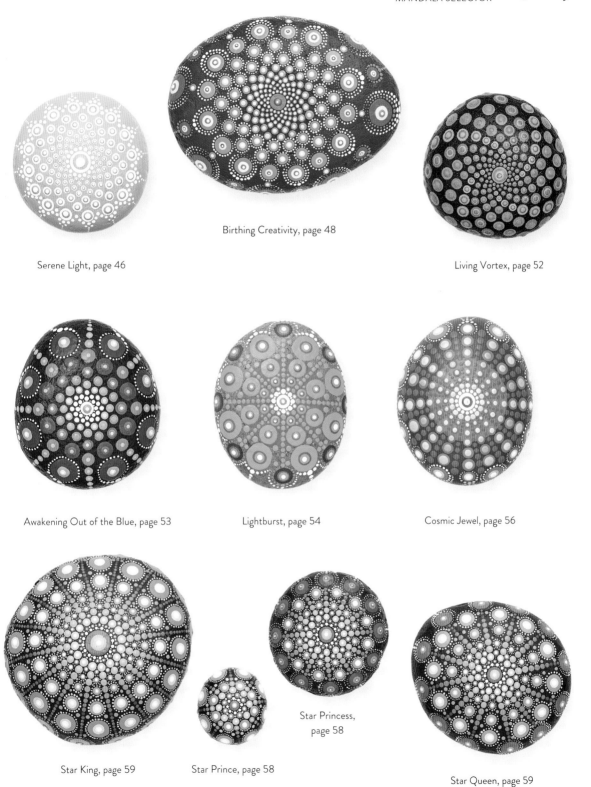

Serene Light, page 46

Birthing Creativity, page 48

Living Vortex, page 52

Awakening Out of the Blue, page 53

Lightburst, page 54

Cosmic Jewel, page 56

Star King, page 59

Star Prince, page 58

Star Princess,
page 58

Star Queen, page 59

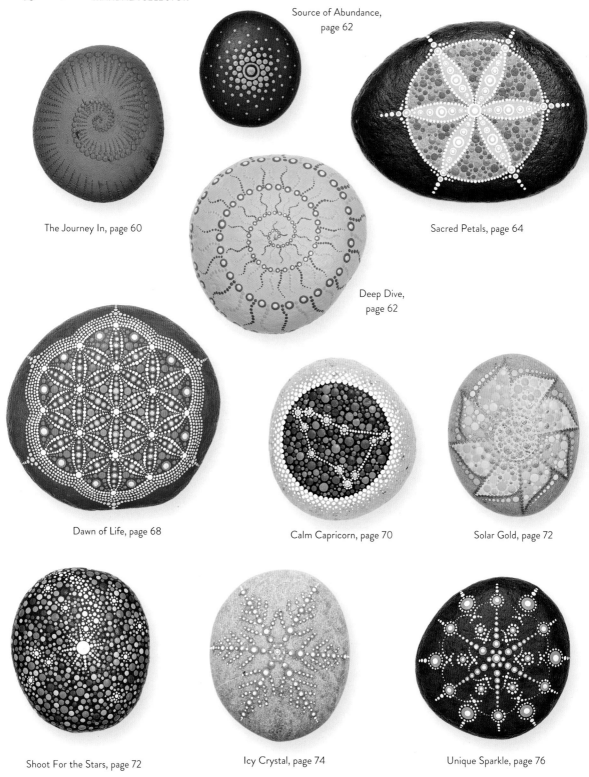

Source of Abundance, page 62

The Journey In, page 60

Sacred Petals, page 64

Deep Dive, page 62

Dawn of Life, page 68

Calm Capricorn, page 70

Solar Gold, page 72

Shoot For the Stars, page 72

Icy Crystal, page 74

Unique Sparkle, page 76

Sea Urchin, page 78

Starfish, page 80

Jellyfish, page 82

Delightful Dahlia, page 84

Purple Poise, page 86

Feisty Fuchsia, page 88

Boldly Blooming, page 90

Dainty Daisy, page 91

Tree of Life, page 92

Tree of Love, page 97

Oak Blessings, 96

The Noble Peacock, page 98

Dragonfly Transformation,
page 102

Sweet Light Hummingbird, page 104

Delicate Heart, page 106

Funky Feather, page 108

Chakra Alignment, page 110

The Golden Egg, page 110

Peace, page 112

M, page 112

Om, page 114

Yin Yang, page 116

Buddha Bliss, page 118

The Supreme Lotus, page 119

Expansion, page 120

Kaleido Light, page 124

The Opening, page 124

GETTING STARTED

This section gives you all the information you need to start painting mandalas. What is a mandala? How do you find and select your stone? What tools do you need? Where do you begin? Which colours should you use? All this, and more.

MANDALAS

The word mandala means 'circle' and comes from the ancient language of Sanskrit. Mandalas are spiritually significant in Indian religions, Buddhism and other spiritual traditions, and are commonly created as a visual representation of the Universe. They are also used as tools for meditation.

A mandala can be described as a unified form that unfolds from or is arranged around a centre. Mandalas can be drawn, painted and created through other means, such as the sand mandalas created by Tibetan Buddhists – they can even be danced!

We can consider ourselves and our world as mandalas; your body started as a circular egg and each year you complete a cycle of life. Mandalas can be seen in a multitude of places: in the shapes of galaxies, shells, flowers, spiders' webs and human architecture, to name but a few. We are surrounded by mandalas and, once you tune into them, it will be hard not to see them.

A mandala develops from 'no-thing', a primal point, which develops through shape and pattern. When creating mandalas, we usually start from the centre and radiate outwards in a series of intricate, often geometric patterns.

The circular nature of the mandala can also be contained in a square, the four sides of which form four gates. However, the mandalas in this book are mainly circular in nature. Images and symbols may be contained in the mandala and we cover a number of these in the following pages.

'To become aware of the mandala is to become conscious of what is going on around us, and it is this consciousness that helps us see our connection to the world and to one another.'

Lori Bailey Cunningham, *The Mandala Book*

A mandala on a Tibetan 'thangka' – a traditional Buddhist painting on cotton or silk appliqué, usually depicting a deity, scene or mandala.

CORE SKETCHES

These core sketches are line-drawn impressions that show some of the basic designs in the book. They show the simplicity of the construction, no matter how elaborate they may look in the painted designs. Similar examples of other designs can be found in the Design Library on pages 32–33.

FIBONACCI

The lines here are the spaces in between the dots, which are implied, but not drawn, in the dot designs. See Fibonacci Glow and Serene Light on pages 44 and 46.

STARBURST

A simple straight line and circle design. See Lightburst and Cosmic Jewel on pages 54 and 56.

GOLDEN SPIRAL

The Golden Spiral (top right) is constructed in a very particular way (as is described for The Journey In on page 60). Here it completes as a circular design, rather than ever expanding, as this works well for transposing onto a round stone.

SEED OF LIFE

A simple but beautiful, sacred geometry design constructed from seven overlapping circles that create flowers (below). See Dawn of Life on page 68.

SNOWFLAKE

Snowflakes (bottom right) have a six-fold, geometric pattern; no two are alike! See Icy Crystal and Unique Sparkle on pages 74 and 76.

SOURCING AND SELECTING STONES

It's important to pick suitable stones for creating mandalas; it helps to know what you are looking for, to locate some good sources and to do it respectfully and legally.

Stones (or pebbles, rocks) come in a plethora of different shapes, sizes, textures and colours. You may, of course, paint on any type of stone, but for the projects in this book I recommend the following:

SIZE
Aim for stones that are approximately 5–12cm (2–4¾in.) in diameter. Stones that are about 3cm (1¼in.) in diameter are great for pocket stones (see M and Peace, page 112).

COLOUR
It doesn't matter what colour stone you pick; you can cover it with paint if you don't like the colour or leave it exposed if it's pretty and use it to inform your colour scheme (see Fibonacci Glow, page 44).

SHAPE
Round and oval stones tend to show off mandalas in the best way; however, don't discard unusually shaped stones – the shape alone may inspire a design idea (see Funky Feather, page 108).

TEXTURE
Smooth stones give a nice even finish, but rougher stones have their own appeal. Stones with holes in can interrupt your design and you should avoid stones with chunks missing.

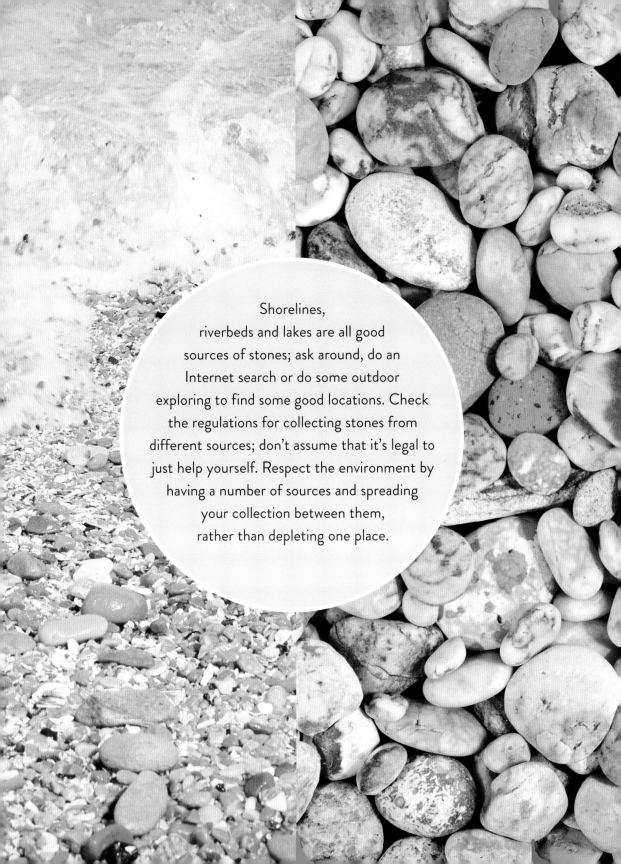

Shorelines, riverbeds and lakes are all good sources of stones; ask around, do an Internet search or do some outdoor exploring to find some good locations. Check the regulations for collecting stones from different sources; don't assume that it's legal to just help yourself. Respect the environment by having a number of sources and spreading your collection between them, rather than depleting one place.

TOOLS AND MATERIALS

There are a number of tools and materials that are recommended for creating mandalas stones, but this list is by no means exhaustive. When it comes to mark making in art – anything goes! So experiment with everyday objects around your home that might achieve results you like.

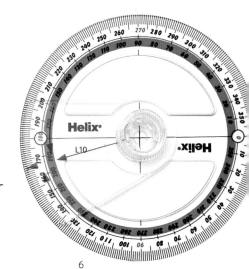

6

GENERAL TOOLS

PENCIL
For marking out any patterns prior to painting (1).

ERASER
Pencil marks can be erased from the surface of the stone or the paint when they are no longer needed and once surrounding paint is dry (2).

PAIR OF COMPASSES
Useful for marking out circles and helping estimate the centre of the mandala (3).

STANLEY KNIFE
Can be used to shave off or lift paint where corrections need to be made (4).

PAPER TOWEL
For cleaning dotting tools, drying brushes and wiping off mistakes that are still wet (5).

PROTRACTOR
For calculating angles for geometric designs (6).

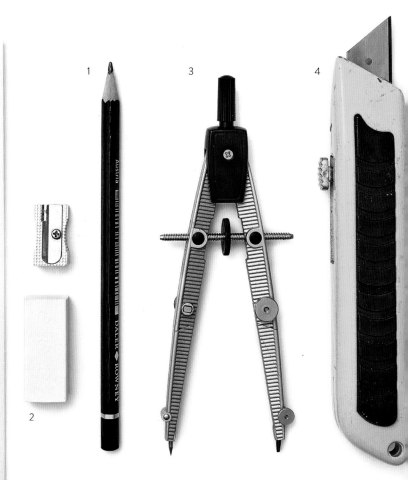

1

3

4

2

5

COLOURING AND MARKING MATERIALS

CRAFTERS' ACRYLICS
Crafters' acrylics are permanent, light-fast, water-based paints whose consistency is perfect for creating dots. The containers they come in make it easy to dispense small amounts (7).

ACRYLIC INKS
Acrylic inks come in a vast array of colours and include a range of pearlescent colours. They are very liquidy and some skill is needed for creating a dot pattern, but their effect can be stunning. They are generally not opaque, but can be used to create a pearlescent coating (8).

BLACK ARTISTS' PENS AND COLOURED INK FINELINERS
Perfect for creating outlines and line designs. Sizes 0.3–0.5mm work best (9).

TECHNICAL DRAWING PENS
Pricey compared to other tools, but give great consistency of line and come in a range of nib sizes. They are filled with pigment drawing ink, either from a bottle or using cartridges. They come in a limited range of ink colours, but can be useful for creating white line designs. Sizes 0.2–0.5mm work best (10).

UV ACRYLIC VARNISH
Required to protect the paintwork on your stones once you've finished (11).

PALETTE
You will need a palette for placing and mixing your paints. One with individual wells is ideal for mixing gradations – see page 31 (12).

9

9

10

12

8

7

11

PAINTING TOOLS

SIZE 1, 0, 5/0 ROUND BRUSHES
A size 5/0 brush can be used for outlines and for creating dots smaller than the smallest dotter you have (1). Sizes 1 and 0 can be used for painting in small shapes such as petals (2, 3).

¼IN. ANGLE BRUSH
Use for painting a shape with sharp angles; use the point of the brush to get right into the corners (4).

¼IN. FLAT BRUSH
Use for painting backgrounds and simple shapes in a solid colour (5).

DOTTING TOOLS

NAIL-ART DOTTERS
Used in nail salons for decorating nails, these give perfect dots and range from about 0.5–3.5mm. They are inexpensive and can be purchased online (6).

HOG'S-HAIR BRUSHES
Most useful are the sets that have a range of sizes. Use the ends of the handles (not the brush) as dotters to create larger dots that follow on in size from the nail-art dotters, ranging from about 4–7mm (7).

STENCIL BRUSH
Look for a brush whose end is larger than the biggest hog's-hair brush, about 10–10.2mm (8).

METAL BALL SUGAR-CRAFT MODELLING TOOLS
These ball tools usually come in sets of different sizes so can be used to create increasing-sized dots (9).

IMPROVISED WOODEN OBJECTS
Try wooden sticks of varying sizes such as cocktail sticks, kebab sticks and wooden dowelling. Try coating the ends with varnish to protect the wood from soaking up paint and needing replacing quickly (10).

IMPROVISED METAL OBJECTS
Try to find objects in a range of sizes that can give you gradually increasing-sized dots, such as pinheads, paperclips and hex keys (11).

ACRYLIC PAINT PENS
Acrylic paint in a pen! They can be used to add lines or dots to the stone. Using the pens does not produce the 3D effect that you get when layering paint. They're great if you want to outline or colour in shapes, and may be easier to control than a brush for a beginner (12).

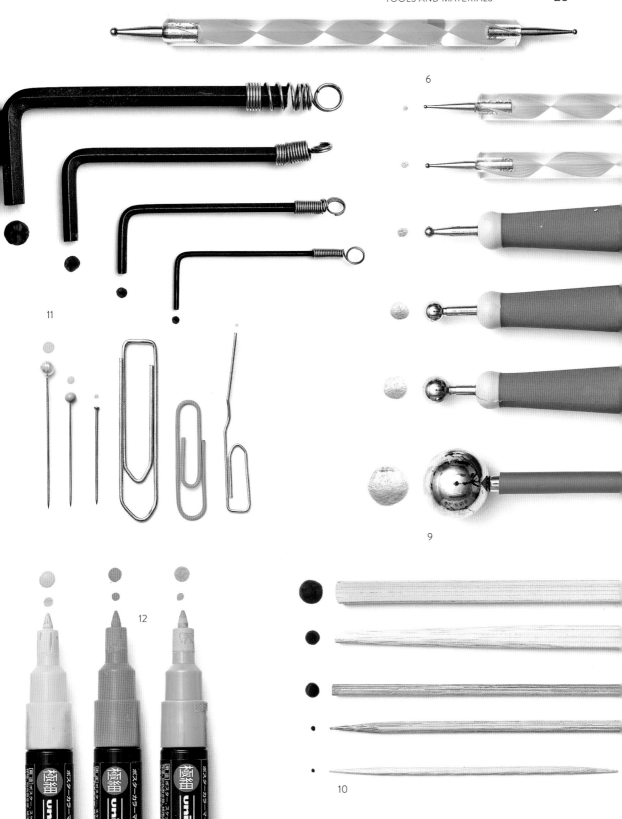

6

11

9

12

10

THE PROCESS

Here is a general overview of the process of creating a mandala stone; although each stone's design is unique, there is a basic method which applies to most designs that is helpful to understand.

TIP
- *Steady your working hand by holding it or resting it on your other hand.*

1 Locating the centre
of the stone
2 Layering dots

1 Wash stone in soapy water to create a clean surface for best paint adhesion; rinse and dry before applying paint.

2 Decide which sides of the stone are the back and front by placing it on a flat surface to see which side is steadier, by holding it and deciding which way feels better, and by working out which side looks nicer.

3 Decide on your background colour and paint two coats with a ½in. flat brush to create the base layer.

4 Most designs start from the centre, so locating the centre of the stone using a pair of compasses to estimate this is helpful (see left).

5 Many designs, such as Fibonacci Glow (see page 44) and Lightburst (see page 54) start with a large central dot surrounded by smaller dots that increase in size as the design radiates out. Designs such as Sacred Petals (see page 64) and Dawn of Life (see page 68) have to be drawn out and then painted in and dotted. Designs with a central image such as Om (see page 114) and Buddha Bliss (see page 118) need to have a centre circle large enough to contain the image, dots and painted shapes.

6 Mixing your paint in a palette with little wells allows you to have just the right amount of paint for dipping your dotters in – between 0.2–0.5mm. Dip the round head of the nail-art dotter into the paint so that the head is completely covered, but not so deep that you cover the shaft as well. This should ensure that you have the right amount of paint. Reload with paint between dots to achieve even-sized dots.

7 Base dots can be layered with two, three or four smaller dots in different colours or shades to produce a 3D effect (see photo 2, left).

8 Several designs use colour gradations, where one colour blends into another or is lightened with white; it is easier to mix these in a batch rather than as you go (see page 31 for instructions).

9 Wet paint can be wiped off with a damp paper towel; dry paint can be scraped off a painted surface with a scalpel and the surface touched up with the original colour. Touch up small mistakes with a small paintbrush.

10 Always leave paint to dry for 24 hours before varnishing to protect the stone. Use a clean brush for varnish that has NEVER had paint on it and follow the product instructions; you can also use spray varnish. Apply two coats.

TIPS

- *Speed up drying by gently using a hairdryer, but allow dots to dry naturally as the force of the dryer can 'push' the paint out of shape.*

- *Be consistent with the quantity of paint you load on the dotting tools to get even-sized dots.*

- *Wobbly stones can be steadied by laying them on bubble wrap or anchoring them with reusable putty.*

The following designs are constructed differently, demonstrating alternative ways of working. Fibonacci Glow is classically worked from the centre outwards, with each row of dots informing where to place the next row; Sacred Petals requires the design to be drawn on first before shapes and spaces are dotted and painted.

PROCESS FOR FIBONACCI GLOW:

1. Paint background colour and allow to dry.
2. Place central dot and then work outwards.
3. First row of dots.
4. Second row of dots.
5. Third row of dots.
6. Fourth row of dots.
7. Fifth row of dots.
8. Sixth row of dots.
9. Seventh row of dots.
10. Eighth row of dots.
11. Three small dots to outer row.

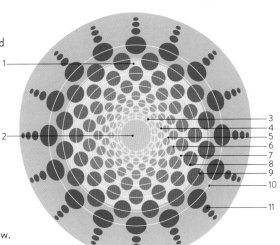

PROCESS FOR SACRED PETALS:

1. Draw flower design.
2. Paint in petals.
3. Paint background colour outside circle.
4. Dot lower centre.
5. Dot centre of each petal.
6. Dot petal tips.
7. Vary size of the dots on either side of central petal dots.
8. Dot petal edges.
9. Dot edge of circle.
10. Dot bare stone.
11. Layer large petal dots with smaller dots in contrasting colour.
12. Finish petal ends.

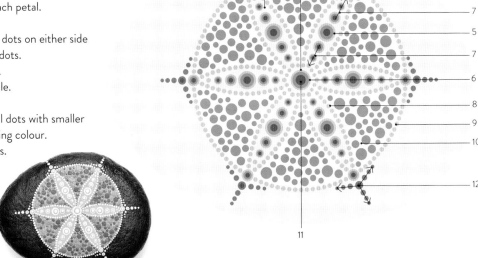

DON'T FORGET THE BACK!

As stones are three-dimensional, the back is just as important as the front. With some designs, you will need to decide how you will finish the back before you start. Here are just a few ideas to play with.

Leave bare to show off the stone

The design continues onto the back

A simple summary

A black and white version

You can't go wrong with a circle

Take the basic shape as inspiration

Show your love

COLOUR

Colour surrounds us and plays a vital part in our lives. When using colour, it's helpful to know some basic theory, as well as the meaning of colours, so you can consciously choose colours to achieve certain effects or evoke certain responses.

COLOUR WHEEL

The colour wheel illustrates the primary, secondary and tertiary (mixed from primary and secondary) colours and how all colours can be mixed from the primary colours. Colours opposite each other on the wheel are called complements (for example, yellow and purple). Those adjacent to the complement are called split-complements (for example, yellow, red-purple and blue-purple). Colours adjacent to the split are called triads (for example, yellow, red and blue). Complements, split-complements and triads are often used in the schemes in this book.

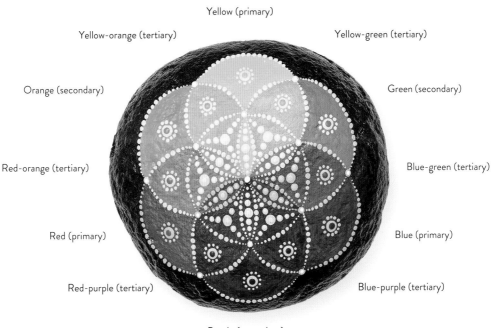

Yellow (primary)

Yellow-orange (tertiary)   Yellow-green (tertiary)

Orange (secondary)   Green (secondary)

Red-orange (tertiary)   Blue-green (tertiary)

Red (primary)   Blue (primary)

Red-purple (tertiary)   Blue-purple (tertiary)

Purple (secondary)

BEGINNER'S PALETTE

For the purposes of this book, I suggest a basic palette consisting of the primary colours (blue, yellow and red) and the secondary colours (green, orange and violet).

Secondary colours can be mixed from primary colours, but it takes experience to mix pleasing greens and violets, and it is easier and less time-consuming to have premixed colours.

USES AND MEANINGS OF COLOURS

Colour meanings are not an exact science, are often culture dependent and can be positive and negative. Here are some commonly held Western associations with colour; however, you may find other meanings if you explore this area further.

BLACK is useful to have if you wish to paint black backgrounds for bright colours to stand out on. Black conveys luxury and sophistication, but it is also associated with death.

WHITE is light and can be used to create lighter tints from any other colour, as well as on its own to add a sparkly look to a mandala design. White is the colour of purity and innocence.

BLUE conveys calm, peace and tranquillity, but also sadness. Blue is associated with water and emotions. Mix blue with violet to get blue-violet and with green to get turquoise.

VIOLET (purple) is the colour of royalty and wealth, as well as of spirituality and intuition. Violet's complementary colour on the wheel is yellow, and these two make a lovely combination (see Sacred Petals, page 64).

RED is associated with action, passion, danger, love and anger; it's intense and grabs your attention. Red can be mixed with white to get pink, which has a softer, more feminine quality that calms emotional stress.

ORANGE is easily mixed from red and yellow. It's the colour of autumn, stimulates creativity and is warm and energising. Mix orange and pink to get peachy sunset colours.

YELLOW is the colour of sunshine, joy, happiness, fun and personal power; it's also the colour of cowardice.

GREEN, the colour of nature, is also a creative colour, and is associated with health, the heart chakra and harmony. Mixing nice greens can be tricky, so buy several shades if you want to play with greens.

MIXING A COLOUR GRADIENT

These are the basic instructions for mixing a gradient from one colour to another. It's best to stick to blending from one primary colour to another, or within the colours between primaries for consistent and pleasing results. In the same way, you can mix gradients of any colour with white, which will give you a gradual lightening of that colour.

Including the original colours this gradient yields seven colours. You can increase this by dividing the proportions further or lessen it by having bigger differences between the grades. Mixing gradients well requires you to look at your results and make any adjustments in the mixing accordingly.

1 Here, I mix a gradient from yellow to red. Start with one drop (or measurement) of red in the first well; continue with two in the second, three in the third and so on, until you have five drops in well five.

2 Now do the same in reverse with the yellow, so you end up with one drop of yellow and five drops of red in well five, two drops of yellow and four drops of red in well four and so on.

3 Mix each well of paint thoroughly and look at the range you have. How do the colours at the end of the range compare to those straight out of the bottle? You want the colour out of the bottle to look like it's the next colour in the gradient. Adjust if necessary.

DESIGN LIBRARY

This library displays the basic structure of most of the commonly used patterns or designs in this book. By seeing the patterns laid out in the form of lines you can easily see their basic shape. These drawings can therefore inspire you to create patterns of your own by extrapolating basic ideas from them.

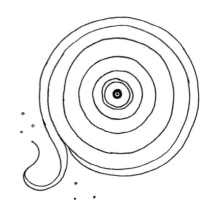

Blossoms in the Wind, page 40

Buddha Bliss, page 118

Om, page 114

Peace, page 112

Solar Gold, page 72

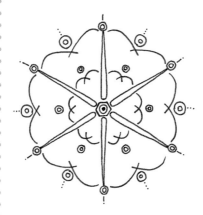

Unique Sparkle, page 76

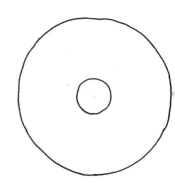

Moon Magic, page 36

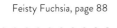

Feisty Fuchsia, page 88

Purple Poise, page 86

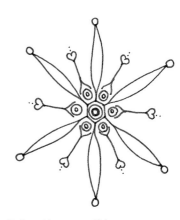

Delicate Heart, page 106

Dainty Daisy, page 91

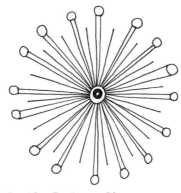

Royal Star Family, page 58

Sea Urchin, page 78

Delightful Dahlia, page 84

Boldly Blooming, page 90

Sacred Petals, page 64

MANDALA STONE DESIGNS

Find the instructions for how to make the 50 mandala stones featured in this book, including a list of tools and materials, paint colours, size and skill level. Be inspired by the colours, designs and patterns, and use these to create your own!

MOON MAGIC

To get used to using the tools and painting on stone, let's start by capturing the magic of the moon, using the front and back of an oval stone.

SKILL LEVEL
Beginner

—

TOOLS
Pair of compasses, eraser, ½in. flat brush, pencil, hog's-hair brush, nail-art dotters, bubble wrap, size 0 round brush

—

PAINT COLOURS
Dark blue, white, bright blue

—

SIZE
9 x 7cm (3½ x 2¾in.)

—

1 Using a pair of compasses, draw a circle in the centre of the stone, about 0.5cm (¼in.) in from the sides. If it is not in the position you want, simply erase it and start again.

2 Use the flat brush to paint the circle dark blue – use two coats if necessary. When the paint is dry, use the compasses to find the centre and mark it. Place a large dot of white paint in the centre with the end of the hog's-hair brush. Use a medium-small nail-art dotter to edge your circle with white dots.

3 With a large nail-art dotter, randomly place several dots in bright blue on the dark-blue background.

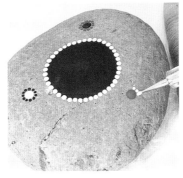

4 With a smaller nail-art dotter, fill in the gaps with bright-blue dots. Continue adding decreasing-sized dots, filling in as many gaps as you can, until the background is covered in dots. Leave to dry before proceeding.

5 Protect the front of your stone by laying it on a cushioning layer (for example, bubble wrap). Draw a small circle, paint it dark blue and edge with white dots, as you did for the front of the stone. Decorate with three dots of varying colours outside the circle using a large nail-art dotter. Surround these with tiny dots using the smallest nail-art dotter.

6 Decide how you wish to sign off your stone in the centre of the circle – I used a size 0 brush to write my initials. Add further dots for embellishment. Admire your work and leave to dry before varnishing.

WINTER SUNSET

Using winter as inspiration, I've opted for colours from a snowy sunset scene, where the clear blue sky glows peach at sunset near the horizon and reflects on the snow. The browns of leafless trees and shrubs construct the background in three shades laid out in concentric rings. Differing colours in the background bring out aspects of the foreground colours.

SKILL LEVEL
Beginner

—

TOOLS
Pair of compasses, pencil, ¼in. angle brush, hog's-hair brush, nail-art dotters, bubble wrap, size 5/0 round brush

—

PAINT COLOURS
Dark brown, mid-brown, light brown, bright peach, light peach, white, five shades of blue *made from mixing dark blue with white*

—

SIZE
8 x 6cm (3 x 2¼in.)

—

1 Using a pair of compasses, draw a circle 0.5cm (¼in.) from the sides of the stone. Draw another circle about a third smaller inside. Mark the centre with a pencil.

2 Using the angle brush, paint the outer ring dark brown and the inner circle mid-brown. Apply a second coat if necessary and leave to dry. Apply a large light-brown dot to the centre with the end of the hog's-hair brush.

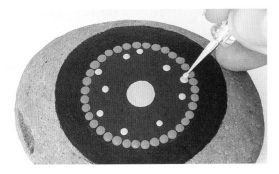

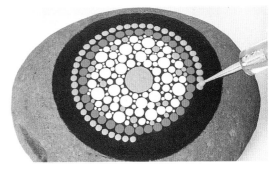

3 Outline the edge of the mid-brown circle in bright peach using a medium nail-art dotter. Place some random light-peach dots in the mid-brown circle with the medium nail-art dotter.

4 Fill the rest of the mid-brown circle with white dots, starting with large dots and moving to smaller dots, filling as many gaps as you can. Then add a circle of small light-peach dots outside the bright-peach ones.

5 With the smallest nail-art dotter and lightest shade of blue, add a circle of dots to the outside. Increase the size of your dotter and repeat with a slightly darker shade of blue. Repeat until you have five circles of blue. Complete by adding a white dot to the centre.

6 When the front is completely dry, place the stone upside down on a cushioned surface (such as bubble wrap) to paint the back. Here, I've used a simple circle design, edged in dots with decorative embellishments.

BLOSSOMS IN THE WIND

One of the things I really love about spring is the blossom, so this stone is inspired by blossom blowing in the wind. Your mandalas don't always have to be realistic; allow yourself to exercise your artistic licence. This design works best on an oval stone. Note the different option for the rear design of the stone – what other shapes or designs can you come up with to embellish the back of the stone?

SKILL LEVEL
Intermediate

—

TOOLS
Pair of compasses,
¼in. angle brush,
hog's-hair brushes,
nail-art dotters,
size 5/0 round brush

—

PAINT COLOURS
Sky-blue, dark brown,
dark pink, white, six shades
of pink *made from mixing
dark pink with white*

—

SIZE
8 x 6cm (3 x 2¼in.)

—

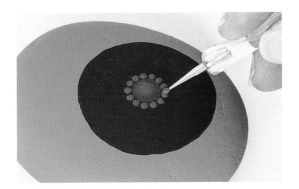

1 Paint a sky-blue background and leave to dry. On the front of the stone, use compasses to draw a circle at one end of the oval and paint it in dark brown with the angled brush. With the end of a hog's-hair brush, create a large dark-pink dot in the centre and, using a medium nail-art dotter, surround this with small dark-pink dots.

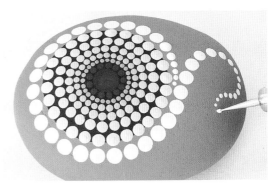

2 Starting with your darkest shade of pink, create a row of small dots outside the dark-pink dots with a nail-art dotter. Increase the size of the dots and paleness of the pink for six rows. In the final row, taper the size of dot where the lines of the circle meet and create a swirly 'tail' of decreasing-sized dots.

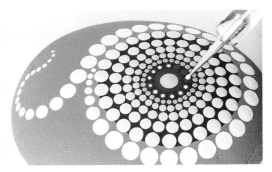

3 With the darkest shade of mixed pink, place a smaller second dot over the central dot. With the lightest shade, place a smaller layer of dots over the dark-pink dots.

4 Place some random dots in the lightest tint around the tail to create the impression of petals blowing in the wind. Place a layer of smaller dots in a darker shade on top of the dots in the outer circle and the loose petals.

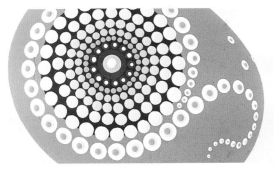

5 With the darkest shade, add another smaller layer of dots to the outside circle and loose petals. Complete with a white dot in the centre and allow to dry thoroughly.

6 Instead of a circle, I've used a scallop shape for the back of the stone.

SUMMER MEADOW

Continuing with the seasonal theme, I've chosen to play with the abundance of colours that might be found in a meadow, where wild flowers have been left to bloom undisturbed. The background is a solid green and the colours are arranged in circular bands, each containing an array of colours painted with a certain randomness, as appears in nature.

SKILL LEVEL
Beginner

—

TOOLS
Pair of compasses, nail-art dotters, hog's-hair brush, ½in. flat brush

—

PAINT COLOURS
Bright green, white, yellow, bright blue, purple, orange, red, pink

—

SIZE
9 x 7cm (3½ x 2¾in.)

—

AUTUMN'S GIFT

One of the joys of autumn is the display of colour that nature puts on for us. I especially love the vibrancy of the reds and yellows, and have picked these out and blended them to bring autumn to life on the stone.

SKILL LEVEL
Advanced

—

TOOLS
Pair of compasses, nail-art dotters, hog's-hair brush, ½in. flat brush, size 5/0 round brush

—

PAINT COLOURS
Red, orange, yellow

—

SIZE
7 x 6cm (2¾ x 2¼in.)

—

FIBONACCI GLOW

The Fibonacci sequence is a beautiful pattern often used by nature herself – check out pinecones, pineapples and flower florets, and you will see the resemblance. Here we keep it simple; but, despite the simplicity, it's still stunning. This design looks great on a round stone. I've used red as a main colour because of the reds in the stone itself – it's always worth looking closely at your stone to see which colours it contains naturally that you might want to work with.

SKILL LEVEL
Beginner

—

TOOLS
Pair of compasses, ½in. flat brush, hog's-hair brush, nail-art dotters

—

PAINT COLOURS
Dark red, white, pale yellow, yellow, orange-yellow, orange

—

SIZE
Diameter 7cm (2¾in.)

—

1 With a pair of compasses, find the centre of your stone and mark out a circle covering about half of the visible surface. Paint the circle dark red using the flat brush; once dry, apply a second coat if necessary.

2 Use the end of the hog's-hair brush to create a white dot in the centre. Then use a small nail-art dotter to add a circle of dots around the central dot. To achieve even spacing, add a dot on one side, then spin the stone around and place another dot on the opposite side. Place the next dot halfway between the first two dots, and the fourth opposite this, as shown. Continue until you have a complete circle.

3 Switch to pale yellow. Use the same-size nail-art dotter to add a second row of dots. Nestle these dots in the spaces between the dots in the first row.

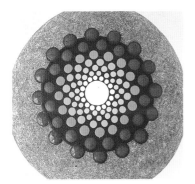

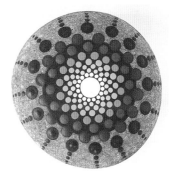

4 Repeat Step 3 for four more rows, using yellow, orange-yellow, orange and red, increasing the size of the nail-art dotter each time. Depending on the size of your stone, you may or may not need to add another row or two. I mixed some red with the dark red to create a new shade for an additional row.

5 Add a final circle of dots in dark red, so there is still space around the edge of the stone. Use a medium-small nail-art dotter to add a row of four dots decreasing in size and radiating from each of the final dots.

6 Leave to dry before completing the back and varnishing.

SERENE LIGHT

Here you're going to start building on the same Fibonacci design you learned with Fibonacci Glow (see page 44), so if you haven't done that design yet I would suggest you go and try that first. I've only suggested two colours to keep things simple, so that you can focus on practising the technique.

SKILL LEVEL
Intermediate

—

TOOLS
½in. flat brush, pair of compasses, hog's-hair brush, nail-art dotters

—

PAINT COLOURS
Tan, white

—

SIZE
Diameter 6cm (2¼in.)

—

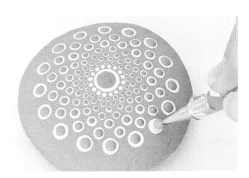

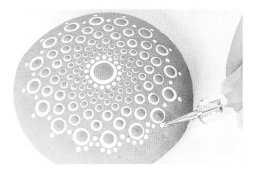

1 Paint the background in tan with the flat brush, using two coats if necessary. Once dry, add a Fibonacci design in white paint (see Fibonacci Glow, page 44). Leave a space between the last row and the visible edge of the stone.

2 Ensure the white dots are dry and then add another layer of dots in tan on top of the white ones. Use a smaller nail-art dotter so that a ring of white remains visible. If any of the white dots are too small to add another, then leave them white.

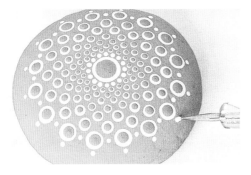

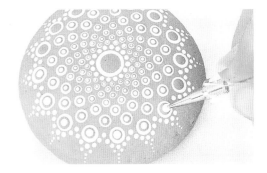

3 Use a small nail-art dotter to place small white dots at the tip of and in between the large dots on the outer ring.

4 Use the same nail-art dotter to fill in the gaps between the small dots with equally spaced dots to create a chain around the edge.

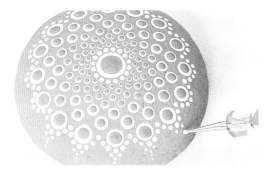

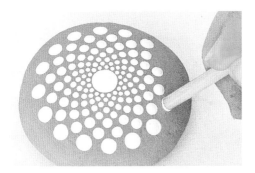

5 Use a tiny dotter to create the design, as shown. To decrease the size of the dots, use the same dotter without reloading it with paint in between dots.

6 Ensure the tan paint is dry and then add a third layer of dots in white on top of the tan ones. Use a smaller nail-art dotter so that a ring of tan remains visible. Dot the central circle in white. Leave to dry, complete the back and varnish.

BIRTHING CREATIVITY

The Fibonacci sequence is a wonderful design that can inspire endless possibilities. Birthing Creativity is an intricate and detailed interpretation of it. When complete, spend some time gazing into the centre of the design. What do you notice?

'The Fibonacci sequence is a beautiful pattern often used by nature herself – check out the patterns of pinecones, pineapples and flower florets.'

SKILL LEVEL
Advanced

—

TOOLS
½in. flat brush, pair of compasses, hog's-hair brush, nail-art dotters, size 5/0 round brush size 0 round brush,

—

PAINT COLOURS
Deep red, bright apple-green, bright turquoise, medium blue, white, deep pink

—

SIZE
12 x 9cm (4¾ x 3½in.)

—

1 Paint a deep-red background on the stone and leave to dry. Mix a range of nine shades of colour from green, through turquoise, to blue. Place a large green dot in the centre. Surround it with 16 equally spaced dots in the same green. Use the next colour for the next row. Repeat for nine rows, gradually increasing in size. When placing dots in rows 8 and 9, leave bigger gaps between the rows to allow for tiny edging dots.

2 Create a lighter set of the nine colours by mixing a little of each with white. Use a tiny nail-art dotter to place a ring of dots around each dot in rows 8 and 9 with the lighter version of those colours.

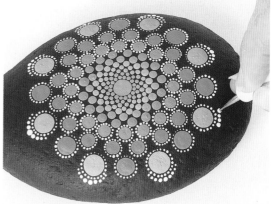

3 For row 10, paint larger dots every other space in blue, leaving a gap for a row of edging dots. Then paint large dots in the remaining spaces in turquoise, leaving space for a double row of edging dots.

4 Take the lighter versions of each of those colours and create a single row of tiny dots around each one using the corresponding colours. In white, add a second row of edging dots to the turquoise dots. For variety, taper the size around the edges.

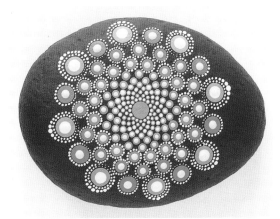

5 By this time, the main dots should be dry. Create a second layer of dots in the corresponding lighter colours, using tools that are small enough to show the original layer of colour.

6 Paint a turquoise dot on the outside of each blue dot. Create a medium-sized pink dot on the outside of the large turquoise dots. Then paint large pink dots outside the small turquoise dots. Surround the smaller pink dots with a row of green dots, decreasing in size, and the large pink dots with a row of turquoise dots, decreasing in size.

7 Paint two more rows of dots around the large pink dots, one in the lighter turquoise and one in white. You may need to turn the stone upside down to work on the edge of the design: be sure it's dry and use padding.

8 Build up layers of decreasing-sized dots in contrasting colours on top of the central circle and the last two rows of dots. Add a small white finishing dot to the last three rows of the blue and green dots.

LIVING VORTEX

Using colour, the Fibonacci sequence can be played with to create a somewhat different look. Base the number of colours you use on the number of dots around the central circle – in this case, there are 16 dots, so I used four colours repeating four times. Alternating the colours in each ring, but using the same colour in each line, creates a swirling effect, whilst using complementary colours really makes the colours pop out.

SKILL LEVEL
Advanced
—

TOOLS
Pair of compasses, nail-art dotters, hog's-hair brushes
—

PAINT COLOURS
Black, bright blue, bright orange, violet, lime-green
—

SIZE
Diameter 7cm (2¾in.)
—

AWAKENING OUT OF THE BLUE

This simple, elegant design, elaborating on the basic Fibonacci sequence, is deliberately spacious, and is expressed with serene blues to create a sense of freedom. The orange, which is blue's complement, adds a bit of zing!

SKILL LEVEL
Intermediate

—

TOOLS
Nail-art dotters, hog's-hair brushes, size 0 and size 5/0 round brushes, ½in. flat brush

—

PAINT COLOURS
Dark blue, bright orange, bright yellow, white

—

SIZE
8 x 7cm (3 x 2¾in.)

—

LIGHTBURST

Lightburst is one of a series, including Cosmic Jewel (see page 56) and Royal Star Family (see pages 58–59), which I have named 'Starbursts'. They have a wonderful feeling of expansion, of something bursting into being, and also a sense of light and sparkliness! There is a natural unfolding geometry to the design that I find a delight to create – I find myself wanting to paint them again and again.

SKILL LEVEL
Intermediate

—

TOOLS
Pair of compasses, ½in. flat brush, hog's-hair brushes, nail-art dotters, size 1 round brush

—

PAINT COLOURS
Dark turquoise, white, light peach, light turquoise, orange-red, dark peach

—

SIZE
8 x 6cm (3 x 2¼in.)

—

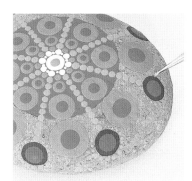

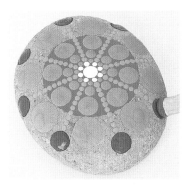

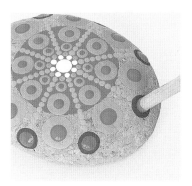

1 Use a pair of compasses to draw a circle three-quarters the size of your stone, and paint it with the flat brush in dark turquoise. Place a large white dot in the centre with the end of a hog's-hair brush, then create eight surrounding white dots with a medium-small nail-art dotter. With the same-size nail-art dotter, add eight lines of light-peach dots from the centre to just beyond the edge of the dark-turquoise circle.

2 Fill in the spaces between the light-peach lines with rows of light-turquoise dots that increase in size towards the edge of the stone. Place the last dot just outside the dark-turquoise background. Place large orange-red dots at the end of the light-peach lines with the end of a hog's-hair brush – you may need to extend the light-peach lines so that the large orange-red dots sit further out on the stone.

3 Once dry, top the light-turquoise dots with smaller dark-turquoise dots (missing out the small dots in the centre) and place dark-peach dots on top of the orange-red dots.

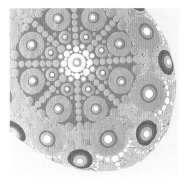

4 Edge your orange-red dots with a circle of small light-peach dots, decreasing the size of the dots towards the light-peach line. If there's space, place tiny white dots in between the white dots in the centre of the stone.

5 Encircle the whole design with a chain of small white dots. Equal-sized dots work well, but tapering the size of the dots creates a pleasing effect. Add a line of three white dots of decreasing size to the edge of each large dot.

6 Place a smaller light-peach dot on top of the dark-peach dots. Fill the gaps between the large light-turquoise dots and the light-peach lines with appropriate-sized light-turquoise dots. Top each main dot with a small white dot.

COSMIC JEWEL

Another variation in the Starburst series, which builds up the pattern using dots that expand gradually in straight lines combined with subtle gradations of colour change.

SKILL LEVEL
Advanced
—

TOOLS
½in. flat brush, pair of compasses, hog's-hair brushes, nail-art dotters
—

PAINT COLOURS
Dark pink, white, yellow-green, bright green, bright blue
—

SIZE
8 x 6cm (3 x 2¼in.)
—

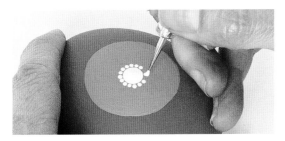

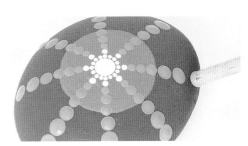

1 Paint the stone dark pink with the flat brush. Mark out a central circle about half the size of the stone and paint it in a lighter pink tint (4:1 white:pink). Place a large white dot in the centre using the end of a hog's-hair brush and surround it with little white dots using a nail-art dotter.

2 Mix a light tint of the yellow-green (5:1 white:yellow-green) and create another row of dots outside the white circle, leaving every other space empty so there are half the number of dots. Use the two greens to mix a total of six different greens. Continue to add to the rows of dots, using the next green in the sequence and increasing the size of the dots each time.

3 Mix a light tint of the bright blue and create another row of dots in the spaces left between the green rows. Use the bright green and bright blue to mix a total of six different colours. Continue to add to the rows of dots, using the next colour in the sequence and increasing the size of the dots each time.

4 Edge the final large blue dots with tiny white dots. Mix up another pink tint (5:1 white:pink) and dot this colour in between the green and blue lines, increasing the size of the dots as you move outwards.

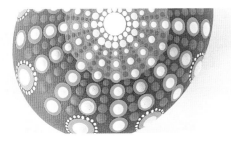

5 Mix light tints (4:1 white:colour) of all your colour gradations and, once the base dots are dry, apply a second smaller dot on top of the dots in the corresponding colour.

6 Add a dark-pink dot to the centre. Create a second row of white dots around the large blue dots, with larger dots at the outer edge and decreasing in size towards the top. Edge the final large green dots in the same way, embellishing as shown or in your own way. Finish with small white dots in the centre and on the outermost dots.

ROYAL STAR FAMILY

The same design and colours can look quite varied painted over four different-sized stones. The finished pieces draw out unique elements, so each stone feels special. As you tune in to each one, what qualities do you notice in how you respond?

This design uses complementary colours on opposites sides of the colour wheel, really making the design burst out in front of your eyes. Following the same geometric pattern, mix more colour gradations as the size of the stone increases. Build the design as you go, swapping between the blue-green line and the yellow-pink line, as each section will determine the placement of the next set of dots.

STAR PRINCE
The smallness and roundness of this stone can make it difficult to handle; when you get to the sides, you may need to paint one side and let it dry before moving on to the other.

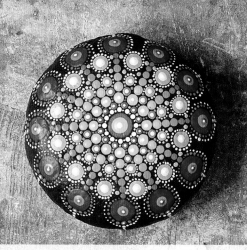

STAR PRINCESS
This stone has a strong red presence, which gives it a warm feel. Add a dark blue in the centre and mix more variations of yellow to orange and orange to red to draw out the star line. Include lots of dots in the centre to tighten up the design.

SKILL LEVEL
Advanced

—

TOOLS
½in. flat brush, hog's-hair brush, nail-art dotters, size 5 and 0 round brush, size 0 round brush

—

PAINT COLOURS
Bright red, orange, yellow, pink, dark purple, medium blue, light blue, bright turquoise, white

—

SIZES
Diameter 4cm (1½in.), 6cm (2¼in.), 9cm (3½in.), 11cm (4½in.)

—

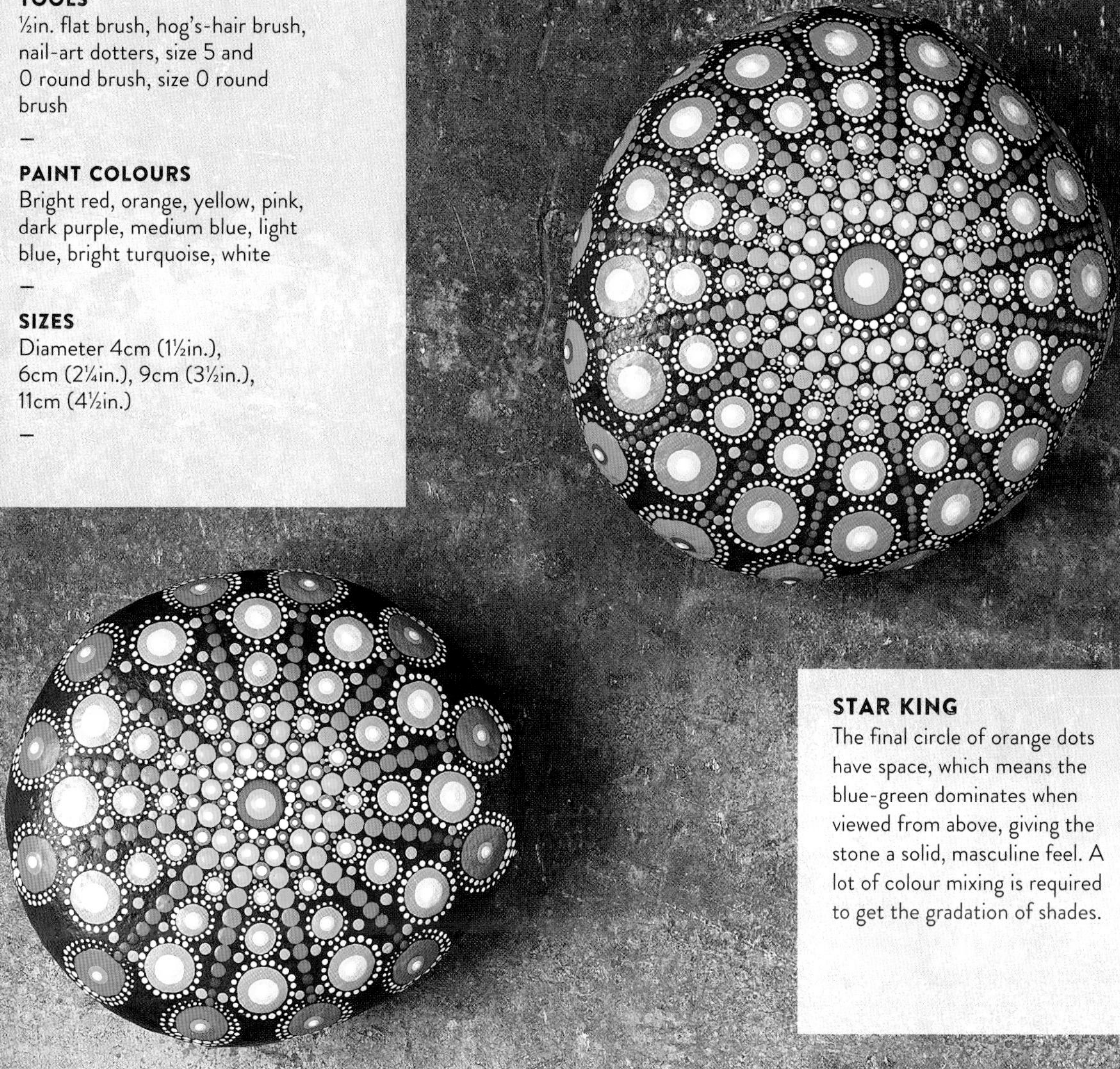

STAR KING
The final circle of orange dots have space, which means the blue-green dominates when viewed from above, giving the stone a solid, masculine feel. A lot of colour mixing is required to get the gradation of shades.

STAR QUEEN
The Star Queen includes a new shade along the blue-green line and the yellow-pink line has culminated in pink. The complementary colours balance one another and the pink gives a feminine feel, apt for a queen.

THE JOURNEY IN

This design is based on the Golden Spiral. This is a logarithmic spiral with a growth factor called phi, also known as the golden ratio; the maths is beyond the scope of this book, but, in terms of the spiral, this means that for every quarter turn the spiral makes, it expands by a factor of phi. However, you do not need to understand or be good at maths to do this design!

SKILL LEVEL
Intermediate

—

TOOLS
½in. flat brush, pencil, nail-art dotters, hog's-hair brushes

—

PAINT COLOURS
Dark green, bright pink

—

SIZE
10 x 8cm (4 x 3in.)

—

1 Paint your stone in two coats of dark green and allow to dry. Start drawing your spiral by creating a small semicircle in the centre. Look at the distance between the two ends of the semicircle. Mark double this distance on the opposite side of the centre and continue your arc, aiming for this point. Repeat in quarter-turn segments. Your spiral will grow exponentially with pleasing proportions.

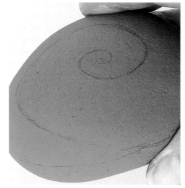

2 When you reach the side of the stone, continue your line around the edge of the stone to form a circle.

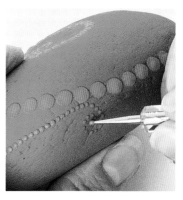

3 Add bright pink dots along your pencil line. Start in the centre with a small nail-art dotter, and increase the size of the dots as you go. At some point in the middle of this 'journey', start reducing the size of the dots, so that the dots are very small when the lines meet at the side. Create a spiral at the end to finish.

4 Create a second row of smaller dots in line with the first, following the same increase and decrease in size. Start a few dots from the centre and end a few dots from the end with tiny dots.

5 For each dot on the row, create an inward line of decreasing dots, using the available space to guide you as to the length of line. Start in the centre with a short line.

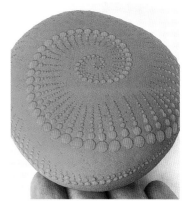

6 Increase the length of the inward lines as you work around the stone, then end with a short line.

DEEP DIVE

What variations on the spiral theme can you come up with? Here I used a tighter spiral than in The Journey In (see page 60) and continued it all the way around to the centre of the rear of the stone. How can you embellish the design in the details? My colours were inspired by a coral reef: follow my lead or have a play!

SKILL LEVEL
Intermediate
—

TOOLS
Pair of compasses, nail-art dotters, hog's-hair brushes, size 5/0 brush, ½in. flat brush
—

PAINT COLOURS
Pale blue, bright blue, white, dark coral, pale coral
—

SIZE
Diameter 8cm (3in.)
—

SOURCE OF ABUNDANCE

The source of everything in our lives, including our levels of abundance, comes from within us, even though it may seem otherwise. Reversing the Fibonacci sequence by starting in the centre with larger dots and expanding outwards with smaller ones is a great way of expressing this. Is there something you would like a daily reminder of in your life? How would you use pattern and colour to express this?

SKILL LEVEL
Intermediate
—

TOOLS
Pair of compasses, nail-art dotters, hog's-hair brush
—

PAINT COLOURS
Dark blue, metallic gold
—

SIZE
6 x 5cm (2¼ x 2in.)
—

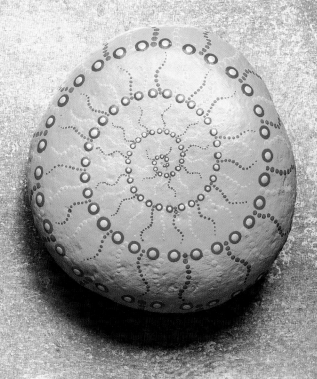

SACRED PETALS

This design is based on the sacred geometry pattern called the Seed of Life. Created by drawing overlapping circles of the same size, you will see the flower petals magically appear. Choose a stone that has as flat a surface as possible, or it will distort the geometry; if this happens, complete the outline freehand, but use the initial compass marks as a guide.

SKILL LEVEL
Intermediate
—

TOOLS
Pair of compasses, pencil, size 1 round brush, ½in. flat brush, hog's-hair brush, nail-art dotters
—

PAINT COLOURS
Yellow, dark purple, white, four shades of purple *made from mixing dark purple with white*
—

SIZE
11 x 8cm (4¼ x 3in.)
—

'The Seed of Life is a universal symbol of creation. Examples have been found in Egyptian, Phoenician, Assyrian, Indian, Asian, Middle Eastern and medieval art.'

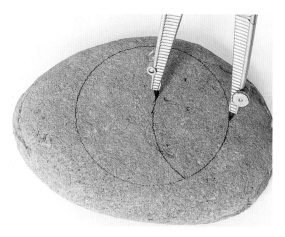

1 Draw a circle with the compasses and mark the centre with a small pencil dot. Place the spike of the compasses on the outer edge of the circle and draw an arc that crosses the centre dot.

2 Place the spike of your compasses at one end of the arc and draw another arc. Repeat until you have a complete flower.

3 Paint the petals in yellow with the size 1 round brush and the background outside the circle in dark purple with the ½in. flat brush. Apply two coats for each and leave to dry.

4 Use the end of the hog's-hair brush to place a large white dot in the centre of the flower. Fill the petals with varying sizes of white dots using a nail-art dotter and dot the ends. Edge the petals and circle with small white dots using a nail-art dotter.

5 Fill the exposed stone spaces between the petals with dots of varying sizes using the four shades of purple. First work with a large nail-art dotter, then reduce in size to fill in the gaps with smaller dots.

6 Ensure the large white dots are dry and then add a layer of dots in yellow on top of the white ones. Use a smaller nail-art dotter so that a ring of white remains visible.

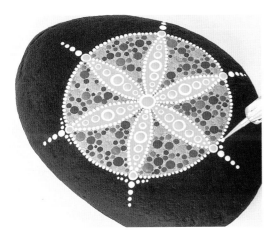

7 Use a medium-sized nail-art dotter to create lines of decreasing-sized dots extending from the petals. With a smaller nail-art dotter, add similar decreasing dots leading out from each side.

8 When totally dry, add another layer of dots in white on top of the yellow ones. Finish the large white dots outside the circle with a yellow dot.

DAWN OF LIFE

In this pretty design, we're using the same Seed of Life pattern as Sacred Petals (see pages 64–67), but instead of one flower we're continuing the design to create a circle of seven overlapping flowers. You will need a large flat stone for this, to make marking the pattern out easier. As you can see, the pattern could be endless; adjust as needed to the size of your stone.

SKILL LEVEL
Advanced

—

TOOLS
½in. flat brush, pair of compasses, nail-art dotters, hog's-hair brushes

—

PAINT COLOURS
Dark pink, white, bright yellow, bright pink

—

SIZE
13 x 12cm (5 x 4¾in.)

—

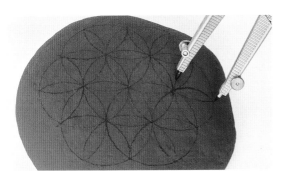

1 Paint the stone with the dark pink and leave to dry. With a pair of compasses, draw a central circle about half the size of the stone. Place the compasses' spike on the outer edge of the circle and draw another circle. Now place your compasses' spike on one of the points where the two circles intersect and draw another circle. Continue until there are six outer circles. Complete the petals by drawing arcs instead of full circles.

2 Using a large nail-art dotter, place white dots in the centre of each flower and at the end of each petal. With a smaller nail-art dotter, create a ring around each large dot on the inside of the design, then carefully dot over the remaining pencil lines.

3 Mix up four further colours, creating a gradient from bright yellow to bright pink. In the centre flower and surrounding spaces, place appropriate-sized yellow dots in a consistent and uniform pattern. Use the next colour in the gradient to complete the inner circle.

4 Fill in the remaining spaces, maintaining your pattern, and changing to the next colour in the gradient each time you move to a new section. Complete with bright pink at the outer-most edge.

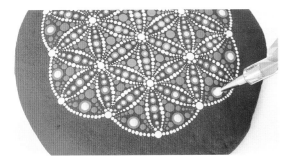

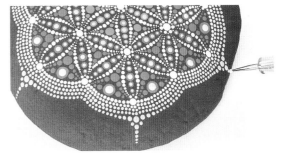

5 Mix light tints of each colour by mixing with white and dot over the main dots that make up the flower petals in the corresponding colours.

6 Use the tints to create a border of four to five rows of small dots, changing the colour each time. Complete with a final decorative border, embellishing at chosen points.

CALM CAPRICORN

I've chosen Capricorn, because that's my star sign, but you could choose your own. You could even make a collection of 12 horoscope stones, or you could draw on the huge variety of star constellations for inspiration. If you love the night sky, you will love this design.

SKILL LEVEL
Beginner
—

TOOLS
Pair of compasses,
½in. flat brush, pencil,
nail-art dotters
—

PAINT COLOURS
Black, white, dark blue,
medium blue, dark purple,
medium purple, violet
—

SIZE
Diameter 6cm (2¼in.)
—

1 Draw a circle with a pair of compasses.

2 Use the flat brush to paint the background circle in black.

3 Mark out the constellation design with a pencil, then dot white paint on the 'stars' with a medium-sized nail-art dotter. Use a small nail-art dotter to join the stars together with a white dotted line and surround each star with its own circle of dots.

4 Dot around the edge of the black background in white with a medium-sized dotter. Create a second, third, fourth and fifth row of decreasing-sized dots, nestling each dot into the space between the dots in the previous row.

5 Use a large dotter to paint around the constellation in blues, purples and violets. Swap regularly between colours for an even distribution.

6 Carefully place more coloured dots in the gaps with a smaller nail-art dotter to build up the night-sky background. Leave to dry.

SOLAR GOLD

There are a number of different ways you could represent the Sun. I wasn't really sure of the design for this until I started drawing it on the stone; creativity is like that. Let yourself explore as you go – you don't always have to stick to the design; you could simply use it as inspiration and let it give you ideas. Notice if you want to go 'off-piste' as you go and follow your impulses!

SKILL LEVEL
Intermediate
—
TOOLS
Pair of compasses, nail-art dotters, size 1 round brush
—
PAINT COLOURS
Pale yellow, bright yellow, orange-yellow, gold, metallic gold
—
SIZE
7 x 6cm (2¾ x 2¼in.)
—

SHOOT FOR THE STARS

Shoot for the Stars is a pretty, eye-catching little stone. Create a sparkly trail using a variety of randomly placed and sized white dots to one side of the star.

SKILL LEVEL
Beginner
—
TOOLS
Pair of compasses, nail-art dotters, hog's-hair brush, ½in. flat brush
—
PAINT COLOURS
Dark blue, white, four shades of blue *made from mixing dark blue with white*
—
SIZE
8 x 7cm (3 x 2¾in.)
—

ICY CRYSTAL

Snowflakes are beautiful, natural mandalas, each one as intricate and unique as a fingerprint. Their geometric patterns are based around a six-fold symmetry (hexagon). Here, I have created a light, feathery design on a stone that has a lot of natural pale blue in it. I've therefore left the stone exposed to complement the design, but you could paint the background in a colour of your choice.

SKILL LEVEL
Advanced

—

TOOLS
Pair of compasses, pencil, piece of paper, 360° protractor, nail-art dotters, hog's-hair brush

—

PAINT COLOURS
Blue, white, peach

—

SIZE
10 x 8cm (4 x 3in.)

—

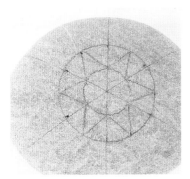

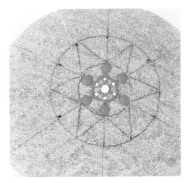

1 With a pair of compasses, draw a circle about half the size of the stone, then an inner circle half the size again. Using the straight edge of the paper as a flexible ruler, draw a straight line across the stone, through the centre. Use a protractor to mark a 60° angle from this line. Draw another line from here, through the centre. Repeat until there are three intersecting lines dividing the space equally. Draw triangles between the lines in the outer ring.

2 With a large nail-art dotter, place blue dots on the lines just inside the inner circle. Join the dots with tiny blue dots to create a hexagon shape. Place a large white dot in the centre and, depending on the space you have, add white and blue dots next to the central dot.

3 Starting with extra-large blue dots outside your inner circle, add straight lines of alternating large and small blue dots up to the visible edge of the stone. Then, using the lines of the triangles as a guide, create lines of alternating large and small blue dots either side of the extra-large dots, up to just outside the outer circle.

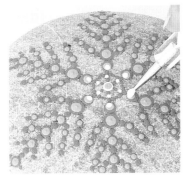

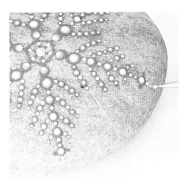

4 Add lines of alternating large and small blue dots from each large dot on the main line, shortening the diagonal 'branches' towards the end. Complete the end dots with a small dot on either side.

5 Once the large blue dots are completely dry, add a second layer of smaller peach dots. Once all the peach dots are completely dry, add a third layer of smaller white dots – place these towards the inner edges of the peach dot.

6 Top all the remaining dots with a layer of small white dots. Finish each long line with three decreasing white dots.

UNIQUE SPARKLE

A unique snowflake 'fingerprint' translated into a mandala stone – there are infinite ways to create more of these! Be imaginative with your colours – just because they are snowflakes doesn't mean you're restricted to white.

SKILL LEVEL
Advanced
—

TOOLS
½in. flat brush, nail-art dotters, hog's-hair brush
—

PAINT COLOURS
Dark blue, light turquoise, white
—

SIZE
8 x 7cm (3 x 2¾in.)
—

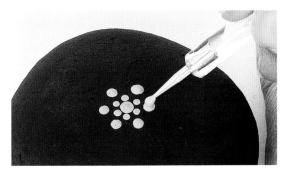

1 Paint the stone dark blue and leave to dry. Place a large turquoise dot in the centre with a nail-art dotter and surround with six small dots. Add medium-sized dots in the gaps between the smaller dots.

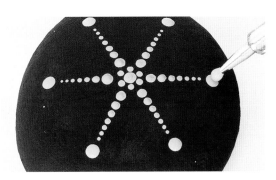

2 Create lines of decreasing-sized turquoise dots from the medium-sized dots. At the end of each line, leave a little space, then add a large dot.

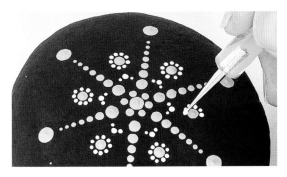

3 Place a small white dot in between the rows, in line with the second dot in the row. Add a tiny white dot on either side. Create a medium-size turquoise dot in between the rows, in line with the fourth dot in the row, and surround with tiny white dots.

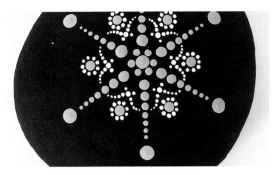

4 From the small white dots, create curved lines of decreasing-sized dots to meet the third dot in each row. This will create a flower-like design.

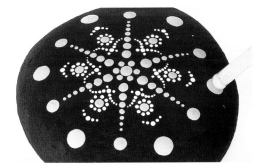

5 Place a small white dot in between the rows, in line with the last dot in the row. Add two tiny white dots on either side. Place a large turquoise dot in between the rows, in line with the large dot at the end of each line.

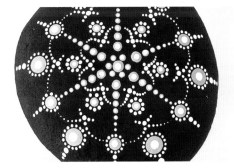

6 Surround all the large outer turquoise dots with tiny white dots. Create a white flower-like design, as you did in Step 4, from the outer small white dots. Top all the turquoise dots with a dot of white. To finish, embellish the edges.

SEA URCHIN

As far as natural mandalas go, I think the sea urchin is king! Exquisitely bold and beautiful, I could paint versions of these little fellows all day, every day. There are a vast array of colours and natural designs to play with. Find a stone that is nice and round, and as high as it is round to reflect the natural urchin shape as much as possible.

SKILL LEVEL
Intermediate
—

TOOLS
Pair of compasses, pencil, ¼in. angle brush, size 1 round brush, hog's-hair brush, nail-art dotters, bubble wrap
—

PAINT COLOURS
Dark green, bright green, yellow-green, white, two shades of yellow-green *made from mixing yellow-green with white*, two shades of dark green *made from mixing dark green with white*
—

SIZE
Diameter 7cm (2¾in.)
—

1 Use a pair of compasses to find the centre of your stone and make a mark. Draw five evenly spaced lines across the stone, through the centre, dividing the stone into 10 sections. Continue the lines to the underside, then join them up with a circle.

2 Paint the background with the angle brush, alternating between dark green and bright green – apply a second coat if needed. When dry, use the size 1 round brush to paint over the joins between the two background colours with yellow-green – this strip needs to be wide enough to house three small dots.

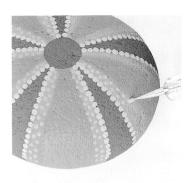

3 Use the end of the hog's-hair brush to place a large dark-green dot in the centre. With the lightest shade of yellow-green, add a row of dots to the edge of each yellow-green strip (next to the dark-green section) with a nail-art dotter. In the remaining space in the yellow-green strips, add a double row of small alternating dots in the darker shade of yellow-green.

4 In the bright green sections, add a double row of parallel white dots with a nail-art dotter. Dot either side and in between these rows with tiny white dots.

5 Use the darker of the two shades of dark green to add a row of fairly large dots down the centre of the dark-green sections. Once these are dry, apply a second layer of smaller dots with the lighter shade of dark green over the originals.

6 Once everything is dry, cushion the stone on a piece of bubble wrap, turn over, and continue the design on the underside. Edge the base of the circle with small dots in the lightest shade of yellow-green. Top the central circle with dots that decrease in size and grow paler, finishing with a small white dot.

STARFISH

The starfish is a beautiful sea creature with an array of different designs, shapes and colour combinations to explore. They're especially good for illustrating nature's use of complementary and split-complementary colours; here, the red-orange, green and turquoise combination provides a bright subject.

SKILL LEVEL
Advanced

—

TOOLS
½in. flat brush, pair of compasses, pencil, size 1 round brush, nail-art dotters

—

PAINT COLOURS
Pale blue, black, dark turquoise, bright green, red-orange, white

—

SIZE
Diameter 7cm (2¾in.)

—

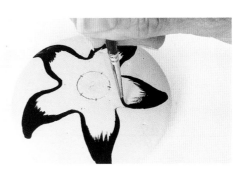

1 Paint your stone in pale blue. Once dry, mark out a small circle in the centre of the stone using a pair of compasses. Add five equally spaced marks to the circle, and then draw five curly 'arms' of equal length around the circle.

2 Using the size 1 round brush and black paint, outline the starfish and add black tips to the arms; feather the inner edges of the tips using light strokes of the brush.

3 Paint the rest of the starfish dark turquoise, leaving the five marks unpainted and meeting the feathered edges of the black paint with feathery strokes.

4 In pencil, mark out a five-petal shape in the centre and paint it bright green with the small brush, leaving the five marks unpainted.

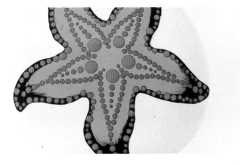

5 Use a large nail-art dotter and red-orange paint to place large dots on the five central marks. Use a smaller nail-art dotter and the same-colour paint to dot the edges of the inner petals, down the centre of the inner petals, around the edge of the starfish and from the tip of the arms to the ends of the petals.

6 Mix a light tint of the red-orange. Add a second layer of smaller dots over the larger of the outer edging dots and over the dots in the petals. Then create some trails of decreasing-sized dots over the dark-turquoise section.

JELLYFISH

Jellyfish lend themselves well to mandala stones and, like the Sea Urchin (see page 78), I have used the whole stone to represent one. This design works best with a deep, round stone.

SKILL LEVEL
Intermediate
—

TOOLS
Pair of compasses, pencil, ½in. flat brush, nail-art dotters, eraser, size 5/0 round brush
—

PAINT COLOURS
Bright blue, deep green, white, light blue, bright pink, bright green
—

SIZE
6 x 5cm (2¼ x 2in.)
—

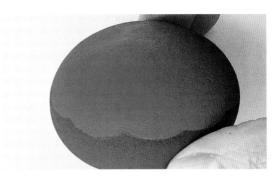

1 Locate and mark the centre of the stone with a pair of compasses. Draw five evenly spaced lines across the stone, through the centre mark, to halfway down the sides, dividing the stone into 10 sections. Join the ends with a curved shape.

2 Mix the bright blue and deep green together to create a blue-green and use this to paint the underside of your stone with the flat brush. Paint the top (i.e. the jellyfish) in bright blue.

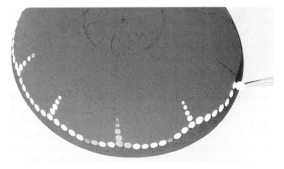

3 Relocate the centre of the stone and re-draw the lines. Draw a circle in the centre, about one-third the size of the stone. Draw five horseshoe shapes on every second line.

4 Mix the bright blue and white to create a very pale blue. Line the edge of the jellyfish with pale blue dots using a medium-small nail-art dotter. Randomly include light blue, bright pink and bright green dots.

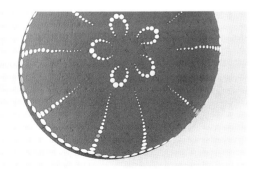

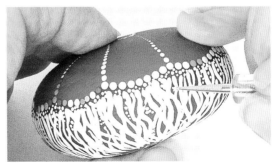

5 Continue dotting along the lines towards the centre with dots of decreasing size. Dot the horseshoe shapes in the pale blue colour. When completely dry, gently erase the pencil marks.

6 Using the size 5/0 round brush, create wavy lines (tentacles) on the underside, trailing off towards the centre of the stone. Add tiny white dots between the tentacles around the edge of the jellyfish.

DELIGHTFUL DAHLIA

Dahlias are such perfect mandalas, as their petals are so uniformly and tightly arranged. They also come in a vast array of colours, with some interesting gradations from the centre to the outside of the bloom. Here, I've played with the gradation of pink to yellow with a purple centre.

SKILL LEVEL
Advanced
—
TOOLS
Pair of compasses, ¼in. angle brush, hog's-hair brush, nail-art dotters
—
PAINT COLOURS
Dark green, dark purple, mid-purple, light purple, white, pink, yellow
—
SIZE
8 x 6cm (3 x 2¼in.)
—

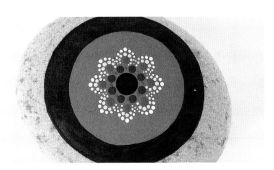

1 Mark out two concentric circles with a pair of compasses and paint the central one green and the outer one dark purple with the angled brush. Add a central dark-purple dot with the end of the hog's-hair brush. Create a circle of eight evenly spaced dots around the centre in mid-purple with a nail-art dotter. Add a circle of dots around this in light purple. Add small light-purple dots to the gaps in the first row.

2 Mix a lighter tint of the light purple and create a dotted petal shape around the light-purple dots. Add a second dotted outline outside of these in white. Make the dot at the ends of the petals larger than the rest in order to create a point.

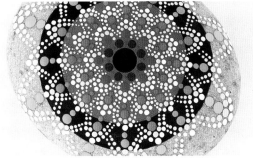

3 In pink, add a small and a medium dot to the gap between each petal. Mix a lighter tint of the pink and repeat Step 2 to create a second row of petals.

4 Mix pink and yellow together to create a gradated shade and use this to repeat Step 3. Then repeat Step 4 with yellow. As the pattern opens up, create larger petals.

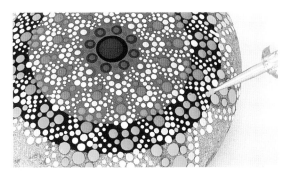

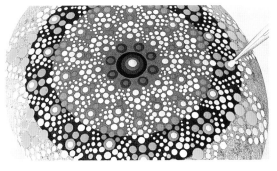

5 Add a second layer of smaller dots to the purples in a lighter shade. Fill in the gaps in the petals with corresponding coloured dots.

6 When dry, add a smaller dot to the central purple dot in a lighter shade. Then add the lightest shade of each colour to the main dot in each petal, including the central dot.

PURPLE POISE

Instead of constructing the flower using dots, this time you will use a combination of painted shapes for the petals and dots for the central corolla to create an elegant, more realistic-looking flower.

SKILL LEVEL
Intermediate

—

TOOLS
½in. flat brush, pair of compasses, nail-art dotters, pencil, size 1 and size 5/0 round brushes

—

PAINT COLOURS
Black, light peach, dark purple, white, dark peach, olive-green, three shades of purple *made from mixing dark purple with white*

—

SIZE
7 x 6cm (2¾ x 2½in.)

—

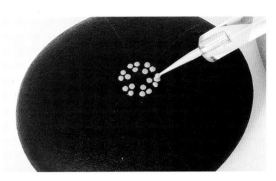

1 Paint the stone black and allow to dry. Use a pair of compasses to find the centre of the stone and add a dot of black paint (this will not be seen, but will act as a guide).

2 Place six equally spaced light-peach dots around the black dot with a nail-art dotter. Draw six pencil lines radiating out from these dots. Place two dots outside each dot in the first row to create a second row and a dot outside these to create a third row.

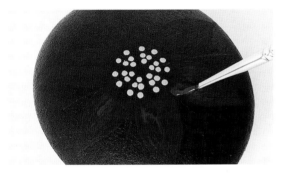

3 In between the pencil lines, draw six large, curved petals reaching to the edge of the stone. Paint these dark purple using the size 1 round brush.

4 With the mid-shade of purple and the size 5/0 round brush, outline the edges of the petals and add a small petal shape to the centre of each petal. Allow to dry. Repeat with the palest shade of purple to the inside.

5 With the darkest shade of purple, paint a petal outline in the middle of each petal and add a small detail to the centre of each petal.

6 Place small dots of dark peach on top of and in between the central light-peach dots. Edge the base of the petals with a circle of small olive-green dots and complete with a ring of small green dots in the centre.

FEISTY FUCHSIA

I have a beautiful fuchsia bush in my garden; every year it is cut right down and every year it grows huge again with hundreds of pretty pink flowers. I love observing the details of the flowers and leaves, and seeing how I can express them as a stone mandala. What flowers do you have around you that you can take ideas from?

SKILL LEVEL
Intermediate
—

TOOLS
½in. flat brush, pencil, pair of compasses, size 1 and size 5/0 round brushes, hog's-hair brush, nail-art dotters
—

PAINT COLOURS
Dark purple, dark green, bright pink, dark pink, white, one shade of purple *made by mixing dark purple with white*, one shade of pink *made by mixing bright pink with white*
—

SIZE
7 x 6cm (2¾ x 2¼in.)

1 Paint the stone dark purple, locate the centre, and, from there, draw four long, slim petals reaching to the edges of the stone and four short leaves in between the petals.

2 Paint the leaves green using the size 1 round brush, adding a second coat if necessary. Allow to dry. Paint the petals bright pink, adding a second coat if necessary.

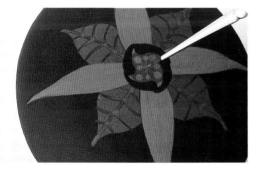

3 With the size 5/0 round brush, paint the veins of the leaves in dark pink.

4 Place a large dot in the centre using the lighter shade of purple and the end of the hog's-hair brush. When dry, take a medium dotter and dot and drag the dark purple paint four times around the centre to create a square.

5 Place a square of dark-pink dots around the centre and join each one to the centre with a thin line using the size 5/0 brush.

6 When dry, paint a line of the lighter purple shade on top of the dark purple in the centre. Edge the petals with a line using the pale pink shade and the size 5/0 brush. Use the same colour to create a second layer of dots on the central pink dots.

BOLDLY BLOOMING

This simple flower design plays with dot sizes and light and dark colours in order to create a sense of depth and movement. Decorative swirls and dot triangles can be used to embellish the gaps; perhaps you can come up with a decoration of your own?

SKILL LEVEL
Advanced

—

TOOLS
Pair of compasses, pencil, nail-art dotters, ½in. flat brush

—

PAINT COLOURS
Dark blue, bright orange, bright yellow, white

—

SIZE
9 x 7cm (3½ x 2¾in.)

—

DAINTY DAISY

This stone is an ode to the dainty daisy. There's something light and magical about this little flower, perhaps because it's a reminder of childhood and that timeless zone that could be spent stringing a necklace for yourself or a friend. Uncomplicated times, uncomplicated mandala: sometimes, less is more. What are the basic shapes and colours in the flower? How can you most cleanly and simply express this?

SKILL LEVEL
Intermediate

—

TOOLS
Pair of compasses, nail-art dotters, stencil brush

—

PAINT COLOURS
Bright blue, white, bright yellow, orange-yellow

—

SIZE
9 x 8cm (3½ x 3in.)

—

TREE OF LIFE

The Tree of Life is a concept that has arisen in various world mythologies – it alludes to the sacred nature of trees and can be used visually to represent relationships. There are a multitude of interpretations; one of my favourites is by the artist Gustav Klimt (1862–1918), and I have taken inspiration from his use of colour and the spiral nature of the limbs and roots of the tree.

SKILL LEVEL
Advanced

—

TOOLS
Pair of compasses, ½in. flat brush, pencil, size 5/0 round brush, nail-art dotters

—

PAINT COLOURS
Cream, tan, gold, red

—

SIZE
10 x 7cm (4 x 2¾in.)

—

'Tree roots dig deep into the earth, the trunk provides a firm foundation, the branches and leaves reach out for light and air, and the fruit is a source of abundance.'

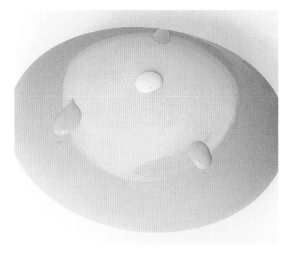

1 Draw a large circle on the stone with a pair of compasses. Paint the inside cream and the rest of the stone tan. Add a second layer of both colours and work fast to blend the two together around the outside of the circle.

2 When the paint is dry, re-draw the circle and use a pencil to draw your Tree of Life design as lightly as you can on the stone.

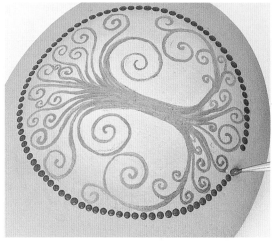

3 Using the size 5/0 round brush, paint the tree in gold.

4 Dot around the edge of the circle with a nail-art dotter in red.

5 Looking at the spaces available in the design, paint red dots of various sizes and create trails of decreasing-sized dots. You can work symmetrically or asymmetrically (as I have here).

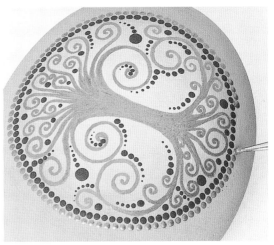

6 Create a second row of dots around the red in gold.

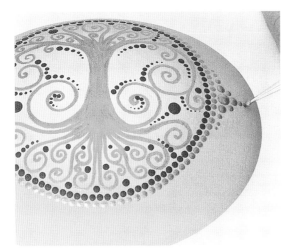

7 With various-sized dotters, create decorative embellishments to the right and left of the circle.

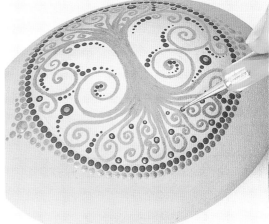

8 Top the main red dots with a smaller dot in gold.

OAK BLESSINGS

The oak is one of my favourite trees, is a strong presence in the forest that I often enjoy connecting with and has brought me many blessings in my life. This is a simple mandala that starts with the shape of the leaf and is then surrounded by contours of subtly different colours. You could try this using a leaf from a tree that you particularly like.

SKILL LEVEL
Intermediate

TOOLS
Pair of compasses, nail-art dotters, ½in. flat brush

PAINT COLOURS
White, turquoise, deep blue, leaf-green, yellow-green

SIZE
8 x 6cm (3 x 2¼in.)

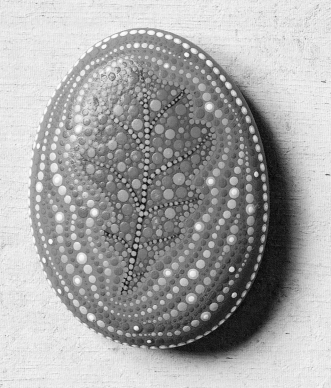

TREE OF LOVE

As you've seen with the Tree of Life (see pages 92–95), trees can be represented with a pleasing symmetry, and their branches and roots arranged into shapes that convey meaning, in this case easily lending themselves to heart shapes. Perhaps your Tree of Love could make a gift for your loved one or be used as a talisman to call in the love you desire?

SKILL LEVEL
Advanced

—

TOOLS
Pair of compasses, nail-art dotters, hog's-hair brush, ½in. flat brush

—

PAINT COLOURS
White, red, turquoise, purple

—

SIZE
7 x 6cm (2¾ x 2¼in.)

—

THE NOBLE PEACOCK

Traditionally, the peacock symbolises nobility, guidance, holiness, watchfulness and protection. It can bring vibrancy and vitality, and help with self-esteem. It is also a symbol of integrity. You can use this stone as a focus to tap into these energies when you need them. Taking the colours of the peacock and picking out some of the predominant shapes in and around the feathers has formed the basis of this glistening mandala. This mandala is time-consuming due to the drying times in between coats, but you can always work on another stone in the drying gaps.

SKILL LEVEL
Advanced
—

TOOLS
½ in. flat brush, hog's-hair brushes, nail-art dotters, size 5/0 round brush
—

PAINT COLOURS
Deep blue, metallic gold
—

INK COLOURS
Pearlescent blue, pearlescent bright green, pearlescent turquoise
—

SIZE
9 x 7cm (3½ x 2¾in.)
—

'In Greek mythology the peacock is identified with Hera, who created the peacock from Argus whose hundred eyes she placed on the tail feathers of the peacock and which symbolise the stars of heaven.'

1 Paint the stone deep blue and, when dry, add a coat of pearlescent blue ink. Leave to dry.

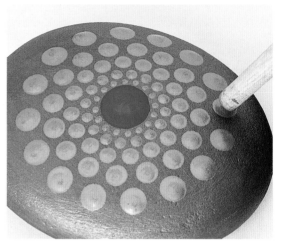

2 Using the end of a hog's-hair brush, place a large deep-blue dot in the centre of the stone. In metallic gold paint, build up a Fibonacci sequence of dots (see page 44) with space in between the dots. Leave to dry.

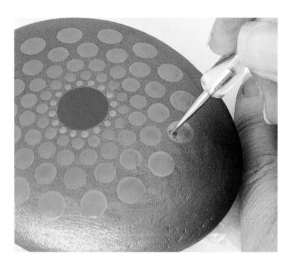

3 Leave a ring of gold dots in the centre and, from the second ring, top the gold dots with a layer of pearlescent bright-green ink using a nail-art dotter – tease the ink to cover the whole dot. Leave to dry.

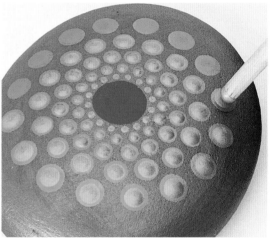

4 Place a layer of smaller metallic gold dots over the green dots.

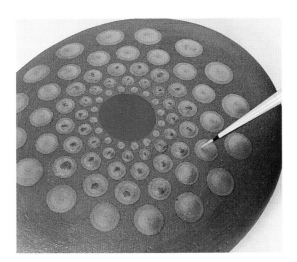

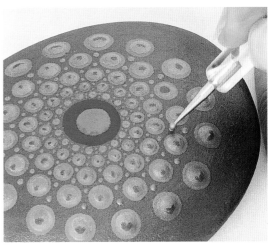

5 Still leaving the central gold ring untouched, use the size 5/0 round brush to apply a small dot of pearlescent turquoise ink to the remaining gold dots – place the dot towards the inner part of the gold dot. Before the ink has dried, add a touch of pearlescent blue ink to the outer tip of the turquoise ink so they blend together.

6 Place a pearlescent green ink dot over the central blue dot. Paint two tiny metallic gold dots in between all the other dots in the design, as shown.

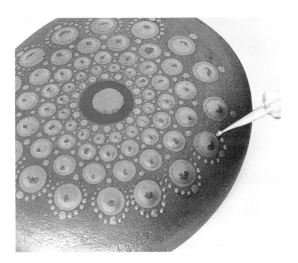

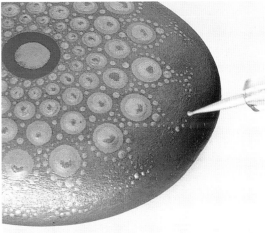

7 Surround the outermost dots with gold edging dots, starting large at the outer edge and decreasing in size towards the centre.

8 Continue the design outwards from the larger dots with two curly 'tails'. Add a second layer of dots to the edge of the tails.

DRAGONFLY TRANSFORMATION

Dragonflies are delicate beings, perhaps the faeries of the insect kingdom! I find them quite magical. They symbolise transformation and the ability to adapt, and bring light and joy into everyday life. Using a very fine nib, iridescent colours and small dots is key to conveying the beauty and delicacy of these creatures.

SKILL LEVEL
Advanced

—

TOOLS
½in. flat brush, ¼in. angle brush, pair of compasses, pencil, technical drawing pen with 0.3–0.5mm nib and white ink, size 5/0 round brush, size 1 round brush, nail-art dotters

—

PAINT COLOURS
Dark pink, metallic dark pink, white, metallic turquoise, metallic green, metallic gold, metallic purple, metallic pink

—

SIZE
8 x 7cm (3 x 2¾in.)

—

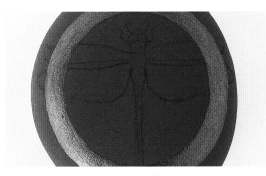

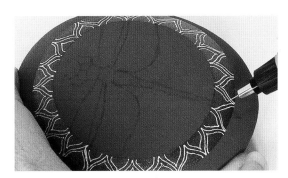

1 Paint the stone dark pink. When dry, create two concentric circles towards the outer edge of the stone and paint this ring metallic dark pink using an angle brush. When dry, draw the dragonfly outline in pencil.

2 Use the technical drawing pen to draw petal shapes over the metallic paint. Outline the inner and outer edges to create a total of three lines.

3 With the size round 5/0 brush, paint in the inner line of the petals with white paint. Use a nail-art dotter to dot around the inner and outer edges of the ring in white. You don't need to paint over the wings, as these will be covered by more paint.

4 Paint the shape of the dragonfly in white, then paint the body, top edges of the wings and main veins of the wings in metallic turquoise.

5 Add areas of metallic green, gold and purple using the size 1 round brush. When the gold has dried, add some metallic pink over the top. Leave to dry.

6 Use the technical drawing pen to outline the dragonfly's body, wings and segments, and draw in the fine veins of the wings. Finish by using a nail-art dotter to dot in the spaces in the outer ring in white.

SWEET LIGHT HUMMINGBIRD

This beautiful, dainty little bird reflects light with its brightly coloured iridescent plumage. It feeds on nectar and in this way represents the sweetness of life, bringing joy to everyday situations.

SKILL LEVEL
Advanced

—

TOOLS
½in. flat brush, pair of compasses, white technical drawing pen, nail-art dotters, pencil, size 5/0 round brushes

—

PAINT COLOURS
Dark purple, white, pearlescent white, bright yellow, four shades of purple *made by mixing dark purple with white*

—

INK COLOURS
Pearlescent purple, pearlescent blue, pearlescent turquoise, pearlescent green, pearlescent yellow

—

SIZE
Diameter 10cm (4in.)

—

1 Paint the stone dark purple. When dry, draw four concentric circles. Paint the central circle white. Mix a light tint of purple and use this to paint the outer ring. Use the technical drawing pen to create round petal shapes in the ring next to the white circle.

2 Edge the white circle with small light-purple dots using a nail-art dotter. Lightly draw the outline of the hummingbird in pencil.

3 With the pearlescent ink colours and size 5/0 brush, paint the hummingbird. Apply a second coat to intensify the colours. Add a small dark-purple dot for the eye.

4 Use the technical drawing pen to add round petal shapes to the outside of the outer ring. Mix up three more purple tints. Use the lightest to edge the outside of the dark purple ring, the next to edge the outside of the light purple ring and the darkest to create a circle around the outer petals.

5 With the pearlescent white paint, randomly fill the circle around the hummingbird with different-sized dots. Place a tiny dot in the corner of the eye.

6 Finally, place small yellow dots in the centre of each of the petal shapes.

DELICATE HEART

When I'm collecting stones, I'm always delighted when I find any that are heart-shaped – what a gift of nature! This particular stone was also such a lovely rich colour that I decided to create a delicate design that was spacious enough to leave much of it exposed.

SKILL LEVEL
Advanced

—

TOOLS
Pair of compasses, ½in. flat brush, hog's-hair brush, nail-art dotters, pencil, size 0 round brush

—

PAINT COLOURS
Dark purple, red, white, dark pink, light pink, pink

—

SIZE
8 x 6cm (3 x 2¼in.)

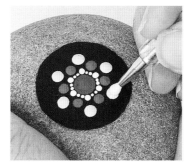

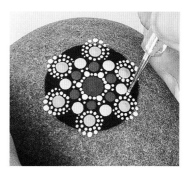

1 Use a pair of compasses to draw a circle half the size of the stone in the centre. Paint this dark purple with the flat brush, and allow to dry. Place a large red dot in the centre with the end of the hog's-hair brush. With a medium-small nail-art dotter, add six equally spaced white dots around the red dot, then two tiny white dots in between these.

2 With an appropriate-sized nail-art dotter, place dark-pink dots outside the tiny white dots, then light-pink dots in between the dark-pink dots. Add two tiny white dots in between the dark-pink dots. Place a tiny dot on the outside of each dark-pink dot to act as a spacer.

3 Add another large light-pink dot outside the spacer dot. Surround this with tiny white dots. Create a second row of white dots, starting at the outside edge with a slightly larger dot and decreasing the size of the dots towards the sides.

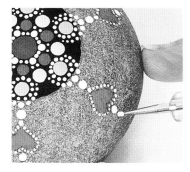

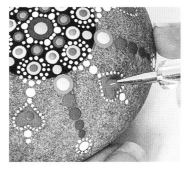

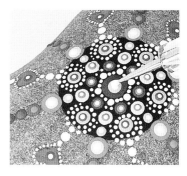

4 Add two further white dots, one large and one small, to the outside of the white-edged dots. In pencil, draw small heart shapes, with their tips at the white dots. Paint the hearts pink with the size 0 round brush. Surround the hearts with tiny light-pink dots and finish with two white dots of decreasing size at the top of each heart.

5 In the gaps between the hearts, create a line of pink dots that get darker in colour and smaller towards the outer edge of the stone. At the end of the lines of pink dots, place a large white dot surrounded by a circle of tiny white dots. Once all the base dots are dry, apply slightly smaller dots in contrasting shades of darker or lighter pink. Apply a slightly darker shade dot to the centre of each heart.

6 Apply a second layer of dots to the lines of pink dots in slightly lighter shades. Top all the other second-layer dots with white, including the centre of the hearts and the centre of the stone.

FUNKY FEATHER

Okay, so strictly speaking this isn't a mandala. But feathers are arranged around a central stem, so I'm running with this one! Plus the stone is crying out for the shape of a feather, and it's important to follow the inspiration of the stone when it arises. There are so many ways to explore painting a feather. I've opted for funky colours and one that's been a bit ruffled.

SKILL LEVEL
Intermediate
—

TOOLS
½in. flat brush, pencil, size 5/0 round brush and size 1 round brush, nail-art dotters
—

PAINT COLOURS
Black, turquoise, orange, bright green, pink, yellow-green, white
—

SIZE
10 x 5cm (4 x 2in.)
—

1 Paint the stone black with the flat brush and draw your feather design with a pencil. I have created different segments that will be painted different colours.

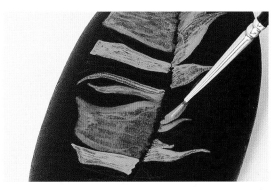

2 Use a size 5/0 or size 1 round brush to paint each segment a different colour, so the same colour is never beside itself.

3 Apply second or third coats as necessary. On subsequent coats, work from the centre outwards and with less paint on your brush to create a feathery finish to the edges of the feather.

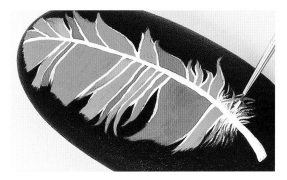

4 With the size 5/0 brush, paint the central stem in white and outline the segments from the centre outwards. Create some light, fluffy-looking strands towards the bottom of the feather with light strokes of the brush.

5 Randomly place lines of dots in contrasting colours over different segments. Vary the sizes of the dots and the styles you use.

6 Place white dot embellishments on the feather, tiny dot lines to the fluffy part at the bottom of the feather and strings of dots around the feather itself to bring some energy to your painting.

CHAKRA ALIGNMENT

This is a funky little design, using the natural, long shape of the stone. The chakras are the seven spiritual energy centres of the human body, each with its own meaning and power. When our chakras are aligned and in balance, our energy is flowing and we experience wellbeing. Each centre is like a wheel of energy, represented here as a series of mini mandalas.

SKILL LEVEL
Intermediate
—
TOOLS
½in. flat brush, ruler, pencil, nail-art dotters
—
PAINT COLOURS
Purple, red, orange, yellow, green, light blue, dark blue, violet, white
—
SIZE
9 x 5cm (3½ x 2in.)
—

THE GOLDEN EGG

The tale of the golden goose is as follows: A goose lays golden eggs; the farmer and his wife think that the eggs come from a larger store of gold within the goose and, wanting to get hold of it immediately, they kill the goose, only to be left with nothing. This is what springs to my mind when I find an egg-shaped stone. I want to honour the goose by decorating one of her golden eggs, so gold is an obvious choice, and purple is also a colour that is associated with wealth. This stone uses a Fibonacci-sequence design with four centres, letting the patterns interweave with each other.

SKILL LEVEL
Advanced
—
TOOLS
½in. flat brush, hog's-hair brush, nail-art dotters, size 5/0 round brush
—
PAINT COLOURS
Gold, purple
—
SIZE
5 x 4cm (2 x 1½in.)
—

POCKET STONES

Pocket stones are stones small enough to be carried around easily, and they make lovely little gifts. Handled often, or placed in view on a workspace, they serve as an anchor to love or other aspects of life that need to be remembered.

M

Initialled pocket stones serve as special tokens of connection between two people. The design doesn't need to be elaborate, as it's the letter that's important. Keep the choice of colours to a minimum – sometimes less is more. Inspiring words could also be used instead if you have enough space.

SKILL LEVEL
Intermediate

—

TOOLS
Pair of compasses, nail-art dotters, ½in. flat brush

—

PAINT COLOURS
Cream, deep blue

—

SIZE
Diameter 4cm (1½in.)

—

PEACE

Inspiring or meaningful symbols can be used to decorate a pocket stone, helping the owner to embody more of that in their life and being.

SKILL LEVEL
Intermediate

—

TOOLS
Pair of compasses, nail-art dotters, ½in. flat brush

—

PAINT COLOURS
Bright blue, pink, bright green, orange, white

—

SIZE
4 x 3cm (1½ x 1¼in.)

OM

Om is an ancient Indian religious symbol. There are differing definitions of the meaning of Om. The explanation I lean to is that the Om symbol contains references to five states of consciousness – unconscious, waking, dreaming, illusion and absolute – and that Om is the cosmic vibration of the Universe, encompassing all that was, is, and ever shall be. It is the all and nothing from which everything arises.

SKILL LEVEL
Advanced

—

TOOLS
Pair of compasses, ½in. flat brush, ¼in. angle brush, pencil, nail-art dotters, size 1 round brush, piece of paper, 360° protractor, hog's-hair brush

—

PAINT COLOURS
Dark purple, white, four shades of purple *made from mixing dark purple with white*

—

SIZE
8 x 7cm (3 x 2¾in.)

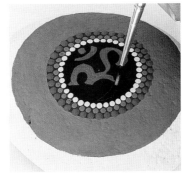

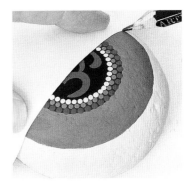

1 Use a pair of compasses to mark out three concentric rings. Use the flat and angled brushes to paint the rings in the three darkest shades of purple, with the darkest in the middle. Paint the rest of the stone in the lightest shade of purple. Use two coats where necessary. Draw an Om symbol in the centre circle.

2 Edge the centre circle with small dots in the lightest shade of purple with a small nail-art dotter. Add further rows of dots to cover the rest of the mid-purple ring, increasing the size of the dots and using darker shades of purple for each row. Use the size 1 round brush to paint in the Om symbol in a mid-purple that stands out well against the background.

3 Use the straight edge of a piece of paper as a flexible ruler to create two marks directly opposite each other along the outer edge of the circular background. At 90° to these marks, create two more similar marks – use a 360° protractor to help you for accuracy. Add four more marks to end up with eight equally spaced marks along the outer edge of the background.

4 With your largest nail-art dotter, add dark-purple dots to the eight marks you have just made. Place dots of decreasing size towards a central, inner point to create the petal shapes. Add detail to the line in the centre of the petals with varying-sized dark dots. Fill in the gaps on either side of this line with dots in a lighter purple.

5 Edge the outline of the petals with white dots. Top the centre-line of dark dots with white when they are dry. Use the end of the hog's-hair brush to create a large dot at the tip of each petal in a mid-range purple. Then create a chain of this colour around the edge of the petals with a nail-art dotter.

6 Top the large purple dots with white when they are dry. Continue the centre-line of the petals with three dots of decreasing size using a dark purple and a small nail-art dotter. Complete by topping the white dot with a small purple dot.

YIN YANG

The yin-yang symbol comes from Taoism and is generally understood to convey balance and harmony. The white and the black represent opposites, or the dualistic nature of the physical world. Yet together these opposing aspects create unity, and aspects of each are always present in the other, as conveyed by the dots.

SKILL LEVEL
Advanced

—

TOOLS
Pair of compasses, pencil, size 1 round brush, piece of paper, 360° protractor, fine-point metallic silver pen, nail-art dotters

—

PAINT COLOURS
White, black, fresh green, sky-blue, bright blue, purple, red, orange, orange-yellow, bright yellow, metallic silver

—

SIZE
Diameter 8cm (3in.)

—

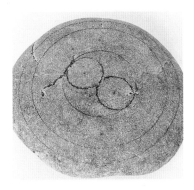

1 Use a pair of compasses to draw a circle in the centre of the stone, then two surrounding concentric rings. Draw two circles inside the central circle and mark the centres. Draw an 's' curve down one side of one small circle, then the other side of the other circle to create the yin-yang shape.

2 Use the size 1 round brush to paint one side of the shape white and the other black. Paint the outer ring black. Add eight equally spaced marks to the outer and inner edge of the black ring – use the straight edge of a piece of paper and a 360° protractor to help you. Then add eight marks halfway between these points to the outer edge of the central circle.

3 Draw in the curved petal shapes by joining the points on the inner circle to the inside of the outer ring and again from the inner circle to the outside of the outer ring, so there is a double layer of petals.

4 Use the size 1 brush to paint the outer edges of the petals. Use this sequence of colours: fresh green, sky-blue, bright blue, purple, red, orange, orange-yellow, bright yellow – this follows the sequence on the colour wheel. Apply two coats if necessary.

5 Paint each inner petal with the colour that sits on the opposite side of the wheel to the colour used for its outer petal – this will be its complementary colour. Once dry, edge the petals with a fine-point metallic silver pen. Add a ring of dots around the central symbol with the metallic pen.

6 Place a large dot of the complementary colour on the inner petals with a nail-art dotter. When dry, top with a smaller dot of metallic silver paint. Add silver dots of decreasing size to the outer petals and the black ring. Create a line of dots to the outside of the petals with the corresponding colour and top the largest dot with silver. Complete by adding the white and black dot to the central yin yang.

BUDDHA BLISS

If it's too challenging to draw the Buddha's face on the stone, use tracing paper. I like this face because of the peaceful nature of the Buddha's expression. The colours used are complementary on the colour wheel (see page 29) and are also associated with Buddhism.

SKILL LEVEL
Advanced

—

TOOLS
½in. flat brush, ruler, pencil, nail-art dotters

—

PAINT COLOURS
Deep blue, orange, white

—

SIZE
10 x 8cm (4 x 3in.)

—

THE SUPREME LOTUS

To the ancient Egyptians, Buddhists and Hindus, the lotus flower was, and still is, associated with spiritual awakening and is considered sacred. Different coloured lotus have different meanings; in Buddhism the pink lotus is considered to be the lotus of the Buddha and is referred to as the 'Supreme Lotus'.

SKILL LEVEL
Advanced

—

TOOLS
Pair of compasses,
nail-art dotters, size 1
round brush, size 5/0
round brush, ½in. flat brush

—

PAINT COLOURS
Leaf-green, bright green,
bright pink, white

—

SIZE
9 x 7cm (3½ x 2¾in.)

—

EXPANSION

Some absolutely stunning and elegant designs can be created very simply with lines, producing a potentially endlessly unfolding mandala. Here, it's ideal to use fine-nib pens; 0.5mm is probably the thickest you will want to use and 0.2mm the thinnest on the surface of the stone. Colour can be enhanced via the background or through the pen ink itself.

SKILL LEVEL
Advanced

—

TOOLS
½in. flat brush, pair of compasses, 0.5mm nib pen, piece of paper, HB pencil, 0.2mm nib pen, 360° protractor

—

PAINT COLOURS
Sage-green acrylic paint

—

INK COLOURS
white ink

—

SIZE
9 x 8cm (3½ x 3in.)

'The concept of expansion is a powerful one. You can expand your mind, heart, experience, horizons, understanding – and, in doing so, expand your universe.'

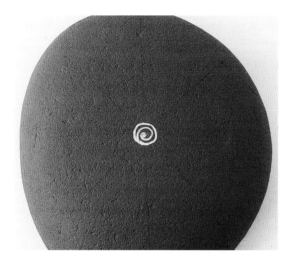

1 Paint the stone in two coats of sage-green. Find the centre and, using the 0.5mm nib pen, draw a small spiral design in the centre that completes in a circle. Using the straight edge of a piece of paper as a flexible ruler, mark eight equal segments on the stone using light pencil lines.

2 With the pen, draw a second circle around the centre and then a number of small curved petals around the circle. Draw a line around this shape following the contours. Mark out dots on each pencil line equidistant from the central shape and use these as a guide to draw pointed petals.

3 Outline the petals with a second line. Mark another six dots in between the petals and draw in curved petal shapes. Complete by drawing a double circle around each of the petals.

4 Take the 0.2mm nib pen and draw straight-line details in between the two circle lines and tiny semicircles to edge the outer circle. Use the 0.5mm nib pen to draw in flat, curvy shapes lining up with the petals in the inner circle. Edge these shapes in similar shapes with an outward facing point; use dots as guidance if you need to.

5 Mark out another set of dots equidistant from the central shape, lining up with the points and joins of the shapes from Step 4. Use these as a guide to draw pointed petals; outline these petals with a second line, completing each tip with two curls.

6 Use the 0.2mm nib pen to start filling in details. All of the petals and shapes are an opportunity to embellish the space, either by copying the designs shown here or creating your own unique style.

7 Use the 0.5mm nib pen for filling in any spaces with a solid colour.

8 Complete the design with shapes, lines and dots around the outer petals, using whichever nib thickness feels the most appropriate.

KALEIDO LIGHT

How many different shapes, patterns and styles of line can you come up with to create a kaleidoscope of intricacy? Anything goes, as long as it's creating a symmetrical effect. When using pens, watch for fastness when varnishing – you may be better off using a spray varnish.

SKILL LEVEL
Advanced
–

TOOLS
Black artists' pens, blue and light blue fineliners
–

PAINT COLOURS
White
–

SIZE
8 x 7cm (3 x 2¾in.)
–

THE OPENING

Take the same pattern and repeat it as the design grows outwards. Graduating the colour from pale pink in the centre to red brings an added dimension to the mandala, rather like a natural flower whose petals vary in shade from inner to outer.

SKILL LEVEL
Advanced
–

TOOLS
Pair of compasses, ½in. flat brush, technical drawing pens with size 0.5mm and 0.2mm nibs
–

PAINT COLOURS
Red, white
–

INK COLOURS
White
–

SIZE
8 x 7cm (3 x 2¾in.)
–

INDEX

CREDITS

The author would like to thank:

Thank you Marc Adams for being endlessly patient, supportive
and the biggest fan of my work, I love you. To my Mum, Kath,
and friends (don't want to exclude by mentioning only a few,
you know who you are!) for all your delight and enthusiasm.
Phil Langley, for your wonderful photography skills. To inspiring
coaches, Oge and Dave. Also Amu, the cat, for our conversations
whilst I worked. To Quarto, for the opportunity to create this
book, and especially to Victoria Lyle, for her guidance and
encouragement. To the mandala stones, for deciding to be
birthed through me in the first place, for helping me find joy,
inspiration and peace. To the miraculous, magical mandala itself,
the mystery of which has been persisting its way through the
cracks in my life for a number of years, until I finally took notice.
And finally, to myself, for having the courage to follow a dream.
Namaste.

Quarto would like to thank the following for supplying
images for inclusion in the book:

Godong/Universal Images Group via Getty Images, p.17
Shutterstock/Cristovao, p.6l
Phil Langley, pp.7, 26
Shutterstock/Persalius. p.14
Shutterstock/Ronell van Rooyen, p.21l
Shutterstock/STEVENSON, p.21r